The Dove in Downward Flight

The Dove in Downward Flight

Roseanne Farano

HAMPTON ROADS
PUBLISHING COMPANY, INC.

Cover design by Jane Hagaman
Cover art by Daniel Patrick Shay

Hampton Roads Publishing Company, Inc.
1125 Stoney Ridge Road
Charlottesville, VA 22902

434-296-2772
fax: 434-296-5096
e-mail: hrpc@hrpub.com
www.hrpub.com

If you are unable to order this book from your local bookseller, you may order directly from the publisher.
Call 1-800-766-8009, toll-free.

Library of Congress Catalog Card Number: 2001095580

ISBN 1-57174-258-1
10 9 8 7 6 5 4 3 2 1

Printed on acid-free paper in the United States

To Rose Salvagione Farano

my mom

with love

Acknowledgements

Thank you over and over and over again to Dan Harnden, who would have hated the overuse of the word *over*!

Many thanks to Terry Welch for showing up with a kind, angelic touch and really great suggestions. And to Barry Alexander Brown and Catherine Wayland Hoffman, I thank you both for the editing advice and generosity, and to Rebecca Williamson, who edited while her heart was open.

To my entire family, who count for so very much in my life and without whom I would be less than who I am, and with love and respect I thank Barbara Brennan for sharing her life's work and her friendship; Dr. William Sherwood who, by his example, taught me more about how to treat people than any book or class ever could; Jan Folta for generously providing me with the opportunity to test my strength and prove my worth.

Heartfelt eternal gratitude to Marjorie Valerie, my talented, extraordinary friend who gently and powerfully delighted in my dream as if it were her own, and whom I shall miss for the rest of my life. And to Nancy Privett for being there and graciously giving me her wisdom, time, and caring guidance.

I also offer deep respectful acknowledgement to the parents of the children in this book, everyday heroes called Mom and Dad, including my own.

And finally, for the kind of love and support I thought existed only in fairy tales, thank you to the person who turned my fairy tale into real life: Daniel Patrick Shay.

Author's note

The idea of writing this book did not come solely from me or any of the people between these pages. The impetus came from those who heard me tell this story and asked that I write it down. I resisted for many years until two Daniels came into my life: one with unwavering faith in me and the other with the generosity to share his talent; one I call my beloved, the other I call a blessing. Both I call friends. Although in very different ways, I love them both and this book would not exist without the two of them.

Although it is a short book, it took well over seven years to write and another two to get it out into the world. I labored long over each and every word, concerned an important turn of the heart would be overlooked or misstated. All the parents and all the children, in fact all the people in this book are sensitive, amazing, and perfectly flawed human beings—not fictional characters. It is their story as well as mine. To the best of my ability, I have passed on our experiences—the few moments we shared that connected us forever.

It is told from my perspective as accurately as I could reconstruct. It is true. It happened. I know they would tell it their way. This is mine.

This is a true story.
Some of the names have been changed
to protect the children and their families.

Preface

While many of the principles and techniques described in this book are alternative in nature, my background is firmly rooted in tradition. After completing my bachelor of arts in English literature and psychology, I went on to acquire an M.S. and an Ed.S. from the State University New York at Albany. Immediately following graduate school, I became a counselor at Pace University, where I honed my skills in the classic therapeutic models and a variety of nontraditional therapies, including hypnosis and psychodrama. I later taught psychology and human resource development at the college level but soon thereafter left the security of academia to enter the corporate world, spending the next five years working for a major financial institution.

Although much time would pass between these career moves, at each juncture, I was looking for more. More what? I wasn't completely sure, although I knew I wanted to better understand the purpose of my life. This ambition led me to investigate a variety of what to me at the time were esoteric areas: the human energy field, the mind-body connection, and all kinds of psychic phenomenon. Intrigued, I read anything I could find on spirituality and personal growth and participated in many related workshops. Most significantly, and most fortuitously, I began studying the human aura, often known as "Chi," in conjunction with the anatomy and physiology of the human body. All the searching, training, and studying came together when I entered full-time private practice and integrated all my experiences into lectures for the general public.

It may be important to note that this book does not contain step-by-step instructions for developing high sense perception, nor does it provide self-help advice. My work, which is continually evolving, does not employ or rely upon any specific modality. It is a thoroughly spontaneous combination of my life experience, my traditional and nontraditional training, and inner guidance—sometimes referred to as "the sixth sense." At the core of what I do is the very ordinary human experience of paying attention. At best, in my practice, I offer people the opportunity to open their hearts and have an internal experience rather than to follow a predetermined set of rules established by an external source. I also extend to my patients a willingness to share a moment in which we meet each other exactly as we are, without judgment or criticism. And in that moment we find a common bond in our need to know that God is in our lives, not as a distant ideal but as physical reality. In this way, I am no different from those who come to see me. I need to feel understood and met, even if I'm less than perfect, even if I'm not good, even if I haven't met the criteria.

Introduction

Fifteen years ago, in the autumn of the holiday season, I sat alone in my office and said a prayer, unable to imagine the events that were about to unfold. In this prayer, which became my yearly ritual, I blindly offered my services pro bono to the next person who called: whatever their reason, whatever the circumstance, for as long as it was needed. For five consecutive years, the mothers of severely ill little girls chose that exact moment to reach for the phone. This is the true story of a simple prayer, a crisis of faith, and the wisdom of children.

But, that wisdom does not preclude the illusion that if good things happen, it means God is with us. If we win the lottery, it's providence; if we have psychic ability, it means we are blessed; if we are smart, it's a gift, and so on. It strikes me as terribly unhealthy to believe that some are graced because they are lucky or have a beautiful face, while others are not so fortunate, and thus lesser-loved by God. Unless we also see the blessing in brain tumors, bankruptcies, diseases, earthquakes and other catastrophes, we will struggle to recognize the Spirit we are hoping will recognize us.

I, for example, struggle with the illusion that experiencing

God will have a certain ambience: there will be beauty and abundance, eloquence and grandeur. But in actuality, the only way I know Spirit is through intimate relationship, contact with people, animals, mountains, a city street, the air, art, music. For me, the key to communion is being connected to, and in a relationship with, something other than myself, and it can be anything at all . . . including illness, including tragedy.

I've long accepted this, known it, and even taught it, yet I continue to wonder if I've been overlooked by God. I wonder every day. All the time. Spirit is not static. It renews itself every single second, and I often lose or can't find the thread of connection that bears the weight of my faith. No matter how often or how much I have experienced the certainty of that connection in the past, it must be reestablished from moment to moment. Quantity does not matter. I can know God deeper, longer, and stronger than I thought possible on Sunday and by Monday feel more desolate and isolated than ever. For me, it is the constancy of communion that is difficult and not the experience itself.

Of course the surest way to lose something is to try to hold on to it, and this is what I often do; I try to repeat my happy moments, duplicate the circumstances. I try to wrap my arms around something that won't stand still, striving to feel it and to prove it is here with me, falling into the belief that "if I am good, then good things will happen." And in looking for help solely from afar, it is easy to miss or refuse the experiences I am having in the moment, including the ones I consider unpleasant or unhappy.

We all have the same gut-level reaction when bad things happen. When someone we love dies, no matter how many times we are told we'll get over it, that the person had a good life, that they're no longer in pain, that they're in a better place, it all falls short because *our* experience is left out. And our experience is that *we are physical* as well as spiritual. Our feelings are the miracle and the grace of what we are. That's why beautiful or logical explanations, even when delivered with love and sincerity, fail to comfort us. It is thoroughly spiritual to hurt, even to agonize, over our losses. Although linear thinking often beckons us to separate pain from Spirit, the capacity to want and yearn for something is the blessing we are looking for. Although we may choose to believe God isn't present when we are hurting, when we are failing, nevertheless it must be so. God is not the exclusive domain of the righteous or the lucky, because the greatest spiritual comfort we can have is to be physically held by someone who loves us. It is simple but not necessarily easy.

And when I'm lost and can't find God? I sometimes look to the modern-day sages whose wisdom and advice have helped me in the past—although, no matter which book I read, the six steps to this or the four steps to that, it only furthers the idea that I am broken and have to fix myself in order to know God. Why can't Spirit be present without my having to achieve or attain it, without my having to clean up my act? The fact is, I've read spiritual writings, studied with experts, taken workshops, and it all works wonderfully well when I am able to connect to life and God, and not at all when I cannot. Why won't God meet me where I stand? Could it be because I refuse to believe God is already here?

Guided, if not pursued, by these questions, the first thing I attempt with patients is to meet them exactly where they are, in whatever pain or illusion. I want them to know that somebody understands how they feel. In being met in this way, in companionship and intimacy, illusion effortlessly falls away. That is communion, that is God coming through. It is physical, it is holy, and it is the result of simply being with someone exactly the way they are without expecting them to change. To be certain, I do not bring God into other people's lives; it is the act of being met where we are that enables us to let God in. Nothing more or less. We don't have to wait for some miraculous, anomalous experience; we just need someone to be there and sit next to us, to understand and put an arm around us. To be seen the way we are right now without ambition to fix, change, or improve us is what we want from God and from each other.

This is the understanding that underlies my work with children. I attempt to meet them where they are. I don't expect them to be good, well-behaved little patients. I try to have no expectations at all. Instead, I roll on the floor with them, beat up teddy bears, scream my lungs out, cherish the eye contact, respect their disconnection if they so desire. In our sessions together, there is no pressure for them to change their behavior, to improve, or get well. No achievement. No rules. This is the place we can meet and be met, even as their parents watch helplessly, wondering how God could have forsaken their children.

This fear of being overlooked by God seems to be a driving force in all human endeavor and interaction. And more than just being seen, we want to be understood and recognized as well. But do we have to look up to find God? Do we have to be good? Do we have to wear white? Do we have to earn the blessing when God is already here in the cells of our bodies, in the earthly and the ethereal?

Duality is the illusion. The physical is spiritual. God is life. The ascent to heaven is inward. The dove in downward flight is the symbol of that communion, a reminder that the prayer itself is the answer.

It is my sincere hope that this story will inspire you to have your own profoundly personal experience and awaken the faith that resides in your heart, for it is the faith of a child.

Your children are not your children.
They are the sons and daughters of Life's longing
for itself.
They come through you but not from you,
And although they are with you yet they belong not to you.

You may give them your love but not your thoughts,
For they have their own thoughts.
You may house their bodies but not their souls,
For their souls dwell in the house of tomorrow, which
you cannot visit, not even in your dreams.

—Kahlil Gibran, *The Prophet*

1978

The recreation room was vast yet claustrophobic, with a wall of inadequate windows framed in sagging curtains of drab yellow. Uninspiring pillars connected the bland cream squares of the linoleum floor to the ceiling and effectively obstructed the view, particularly for those in the back. The room had originally been set up lecture-style, with folding chairs lined up in neat rows, but the students had added their personal touch by pulling stuffed orange lounge furniture up to the front. By the time I reached the makeshift stage—a six-foot platform—the place was packed with students, who were even balanced on the backs of the chairs and sofas or lying on the floor in front.

Even though I had experience giving these lecture-demonstrations, I was anxious; my mother was sitting in the front row. As usual, I began with an overview of the subject, defining the technical terms and outlining the basics, including a series of simple exercises that the audience could use to determine their susceptibility and for purposes of self-hypnosis. Introduction complete, I invited questions from the audience to get a sense of what they knew about hypnosis and what, if any, misconceptions they may have held. As soon as I got into the rhythm of interaction, my nervousness dissipated.

Before beginning the hypnotic induction, I told those who did not wish to participate to ignore my ensuing instructions. Assured the parameters were sufficiently understood, I gave the induction to the entire room and then asked everyone to extend an arm. I quickly performed another induction, reinforcing the rigidity of the extended arms, suggesting they were made of steel. Walking through the audience, testing the outstretched arms, it was easy to determine who was truly somnambulistic (in a deep trance state).

About half the audience knew they weren't hypnotized and lowered their arms without instruction as I moved through the room. Many pretended to be hypnotized, making an enormous effort to hold their arms rigid. I knew from experience that this was usually not done as a deception but out of a genuine desire to be hypnotized. When all was said and done, as was typical, about ten percent of those present were in a deep hypnotic state.

I touched the arms of those who weren't somnambulistic and whispered, "Come back to the room, present and fully awake." By the end of this process, about fifteen people were still holding their arms out, stiff as boards. I quickly narrowed the group down to the three that, when asked, were most eager to come to the front of the room.

Two men and a young woman came forward. I approached each of them and whispered, "Nothing that happens in this room will disturb you. You can hear only the sound of my voice." I already knew that the young woman was the perfect subject for the demonstration. Her name was Heather; she was a student and a member of a peer-counseling group I was supervising. During a private session, she confided that she had asthma, the attacks increasingly affecting her life—especially when it came to sports. Our relationship had deepened and finally, one afternoon, I asked her if she could recall her first asthma attack.

"No, I never really thought about it before," she responded. "But now that you ask, I can't remember ever not having asthma attacks."

"If you're willing, we could try hypnosis to see if we can find that first episode."

"Really?"

I explained this was a standard procedure in hypnotic therapy. "The idea is to have a person go back in time to look for the original onset of the condition that's troubling them."

"What good does that do?"

"Well, sometimes the body remembers things the mind does not recall. And if we can find that memory, there's a chance we can release it."

"Can we do it now?"

I was surprised at what a good subject she was and how quickly she went into a deep somnambulistic sleep. I led her through an age-regression, rolling back her memory, but we were unable to locate the first attack. She appeared to have been suffering from the illness all her life and was displaying symptoms as early as infancy. When we reached her actual birth, to my surprise, she began crying like a newborn and gasping for air. Between sobs, she described a room filled with bright lights and activity.

"I can hear them talking," Heather said. "Someone is saying 'the cord is wrapped around the baby's neck.' "

In the next moment, to my horror, Heather appeared to be in severe respiratory distress and seconds later her lips actually started to turn blue. Assuming this could be her first asthma attack, I immediately brought her forward in time until her normal breathing returned, making certain she was all right. She assured me she was and reiterated her desire to continue the process. I carefully altered the induction and returned her to her birth, hoping she could go through the experience without revisiting the symptoms.

One breath at a time, Heather started reliving her birth,

describing it in detail, her breathing increasingly labored the closer she got to the moment of delivery.

"It's okay, you can breathe freely and easily."

Heather continued to wheeze.

"Take a deep breath . . . okay, now another. Good, you're doing great, you can breathe freely and easily. Take one breath at a time. Slow, easy breaths."

It took about twenty minutes before she was able to go through the birth process without any respiratory trauma. Before waking her, in order to increase the probability the suggestions would hold, I told her she would not remember any of what happened during the session. Upon waking, she remembered nothing but said she felt fine, good in fact. "Did it work?" she asked.

Two weeks later she walked into my office, sat down, and said, "I just ran two miles without a wheeze. I'm ready to remember everything."

I played her the tape of the previous session and she sat listening, enraptured. Afterwards, Heather was anxious to talk to her mother, who confirmed the accuracy of her account. Although it is not always so dramatic, Heather didn't have another attack for the rest of the time I knew her, which amounted to years, years in which she added many new activities to her life, in addition to running. I suppose the point here is that the phenomenon of hypnosis is less important than the material uncovered in the process and what is done about it.

To have a breakthrough of such a dynamic nature, Heather clearly had the predilection for deep trance work, but no more so than the man sitting on the edge of the stage area. He was not among the three I chose for the demonstration. Somewhat older than the others, his name was Ryan, and I recognized him as a colleague's boyfriend. Although I was not about to use him in the demonstration, he was by far the best subject in the room and I knew it without having to test his arm.

Although he was not someone I knew very well, I had seen

him being inappropriately flirtatious at several faculty parties, which left me feeling vaguely ill at ease. Uncomfortable with this, and the idea of working with a colleague's boyfriend in front of an audience largely composed of students, I led him through a hushed conversation, my back to the room.

"Ryan, at the count of three you'll be wide awake and fully present. One, waking up. Two, feeling alert. Three, wide awake."

"Are you feeling all right?" I asked.

"Yeah, but I want to be hypnotized."

"Well, you were." He was as deeply under as anyone I'd ever seen.

"No way."

"Is there a particular reason you want to be hypnotized?"

"I think it might help."

"With what?"

"My dreams."

I had no idea what he meant by that, and I didn't want to find out under these circumstances. It would have been like stepping into a puddle of unknown depth.

"Why don't you call my office and set up an appointment?"

"Okay."

"Fine."

I returned to the stage and asked the three students who were still hypnotized to lift their heads and open their eyes while remaining deep asleep. In the audience, Ryan slipped back under at the sound of my voice, extraordinarily gifted from one point of view, susceptible from another. I touched each of the students lightly on the forehead and reinforced the suggestion that their arms were stiff as steel. Lining them up next to me, I asked the strongest-looking guy in the room to join us on stage and also hold his arm out taut. Determined to prove his virility, he strained to hold his arm rigid as, one by one, members of the audience came up and tried to push it down. The same audience members then tested the outstretched arms of the three hyp-notized volunteers for comparison and all readily acknowl-edged the striking difference between a person who was straining to hold his arm stiff and a person who believed his or her arm was made of steel.

After a series of demonstrations, including several that exemplified how the mind processed certain positive and neg-ative versions of language cues, I woke the subjects with the suggestion that they could remember everything they had said and done while on stage. Then I invited the audience to ask them questions about their experience. When asked if they were aware of their behavior during the demonstration, all three had the same response, the one I'd come to expect: they absolutely knew what was going on, they knew they were holding their arms out and felt they could have lowered them if they wanted to. All three had difficulty believing they were hypnotized at all. After a full hour of demonstration, the audi-ence found their incredulity humorous. With everyone laugh-ing, it seemed a good place to end the evening. I caught my mother's eye as I left the stage; the look on her face was the only review that mattered.

Ryan came to my office two weeks later. He told me he'd been having a series of disturbing, prophetic dreams, claiming three of them, all horrific tragedies, had come to pass. In searching for what could be triggering his dreams, he began telling me about the more personal aspects of his life, includ-ing the fact that he had been unfaithful to his live-in girlfriend, with whom I had a professional relationship. I wanted to steer him back to the subject at hand, uncomfortable with the dis-crepancy between his considerable psychic talent and his per-sonal ethics, so I asked him to return to recounting his dreams.

He said that while under, during the demonstration, he felt unusually in touch with his psychic vision—although he didn't use those words—and thought that hypnosis might help him gain some level of control over it. He told me that several of his "dreams" had prompted him to warn people he knew, often at a distance, and claimed they were then able to avoid what turned out to be very real danger. In fact, he confided, it was the consequence of ignoring one of his premonitions and failing to warn a close friend, who was later caught in a fire, that prompted his approaching me for help. He actually broke down at one point as he recounted these experiences, and it was obvious his desperation was real.

"These are not normal nightmares. These come true," he said. "They frighten me and I just want them to stop."

"Can you tell when you're going to have one? Have you noticed any warning signs?"

"No. That's why I'm afraid to go to sleep, there's no way to tell. It just happens."

"What happens?"

"I fall asleep normally and there are these swirling colors. It's hard to explain. It's like being in a kaleidoscope. And then a picture with supersharp images and colors comes into focus, and it's usually something awful like someone having a heart attack, or a plane crash, or something like that. I wake up in a cold sweat because I recognize the people in the dreams and feel obligated to warn them, which makes me feel, and probably look, ridiculous—plus, I can't get a good night's sleep. I just want the visions to stop."

Before encountering Ryan, it never occurred to me that someone might want to rid themselves of psychic abilities, abilities I assumed to be a gift. Appearing foolish seemed a small price to pay for the opportunity to save someone's life, but for Ryan, second sight was anything but a blessing, it was a nightly curse, the constant fear of what sleep might bring.

The further we got into the session the more I began to trust his dreams even though I didn't completely trust him. Having already confided that he had cheated on his girlfriend, he seemed all the more cavalier because of his flirtatiousness. It was a peculiar situation that challenged my long-held belief that one had to be pure of heart, highly evolved, or enlightened to possess clairvoyant abilities. He seemed an unlikely candidate for such a gift.

Ryan and I had only the one session together and weren't very deep into our exploration when a potentially tragic situation occurred close to home. A good friend, as upset as I'd ever heard her, called to tell me her sister's children had been abducted. By the time Ryan and I met again in my office, an idea had emerged. "Since we don't know what's triggering these precognitive dreams or how to stop them from recurring, I'd like to try something. Maybe we could induce one of these dreams."

"You mean deliberately bring one on?" Ryan snapped, the agitation of panic in his voice. "That's the opposite of what I want."

"If your goal is to stop them, then maybe you have to first learn to control them."

Ryan looked doubtful. "I don't like to see bad things."

"I understand, but this time it won't be unexpected, it won't be at night, and you won't be alone. Maybe we can use your abilities to avoid another disaster."

I told him about the missing children and, skeptically, he agreed to give it a try. He went under right away. "Where are you?" I asked.

"In the place where the colors are."

I told him the names of the missing children, described them as best I could, and then realized I didn't have enough information to ask useful questions. I stuck to the basics.

"Are they alive?"

"Yes."

"Are they alone?"

"No, I think somebody's with them."

"Is it dark? Are they frightened? Are they inside, outside? Describe what it looks like, tell me what you see."

Out of context, his responses seemed of little use. Later

that evening I called my friend back and told her about Ryan's dreams. Grateful for any help in locating the children, she was open to this approach. I told her I needed all the information she had about the children's disappearance and questioned her in detail, meticulously jotting down everything she said.

The next time Ryan and I got together, I was better prepared. Knowing that the father of the missing children was the primary suspect in the kidnapping and his haunts not altogether unknown, I spread out a map of the area in question and asked Ryan to point out the location of the children. He wasn't able to make sense of the map, so I took a more active role.

"Are they close to here?" I said, pointing to a particular locale.

He shook his head.

"How about here?"

He shook his head again.

"And here?"

"No."

"Then here?"

"Yes."

After about an hour and a half of this, a picture began to emerge and I was able to draw a small triangle on the map where, according to Ryan, the children could be found. After the session, I called my friend. "This is what we got: they're alive, they're in a wooded area not that far away from you and with someone they know, probably a man. We think they're in a cabin near an old gas station. The pump has one of those glass balls on top of it with the word 'gas' written on it as opposed to a brand name. There's also a small grocery store or something similar across the street." Some of the information was verbatim from Ryan, some inferred.

After we spoke, my friend called her sister and passed the information on. The children's mother immediately knew which gas station we were referring to and said the children had just been found in that area. She also said that this is what she'd been telling the police all along. Both the children were fine. They'd been with their father who had used his credit card at the grocery store Ryan described—which was how they zeroed in on his location.

The cabin the children were found in was right in the middle of the triangle Ryan and I had drawn, but all we had done was confirm what apparently everybody else already knew. In no way were we responsible for finding the children and no one was particularly impressed with our work. Even I wasn't sure how to tell if what Ryan saw was fact, fiction, or suggestion. But some good did come of it: he learned to hypnotize himself and, in doing so, gained the confidence he needed to take control of his abilities rather than be terrorized by them. With a new sense of self-assurance he could guide his own inner experience without assistance. He said he'd call if he needed help. He never did.

I don't know what became of Ryan. I don't know if he continued to utilize his abilities, or even grew to appreciate them, but I came away from the experience with a different concept of high sense perception. What I previously assumed to be a rare ability reserved for the "good" or "pious," a gift bestowed upon a special chosen few turned out to be a natural part of the human experience . . . including mine.

PART ONE

Hope

Margaret

1

Jesus loves me, this I know
For the Bible tells me so
Little ones to him belong
They are weak but he is strong
Yes, Jesus loves me
Yes, Jesus loves me
Yes, Jesus loves me
The Bible tells me so.

From the hymn, *Jesus Loves Me,*
words by Anna B. Warner

Margaret opened her eyes, and the first thing she saw was the pink canopy above her. She was used to seeing it floating over the bed and often fell asleep imagining all sorts of images in its fabric. Rolling over onto her side, she was confronted by a small army of stuffed animals and dolls. It was not her usual inclination to play with them, preferring to spend most of her free time reading and watching videos, but she liked having them around just the same and reached out to pat the friendly-looking lion on his head before bounding to the floor, drawn by the sounds of life coming from the kitchen. It was Saturday, no school today.

Margaret certainly wasn't disappointed to have the day off, but would have been just as happy if it were a school day. She began attending nursery school when she was three and kindergarten when she was five. Now in the first grade, she eagerly looked forward to weekday mornings and the company of her classmates. She would normally sit quietly and watch them play from over the top of whatever book she was reading, rarely joining in, her popularity not adversely affected by her choice to remain on the sidelines. In short order, in good order, she always returned to her studies. No one was surprised when she scored exceptionally high on her reading tests.

She and her family lived in a small suburban community twenty miles north of New York City. Her parents, Teresa and Mark, commuted to nearby jobs and, although she was only six years old, Margaret was comfortable with a certain amount of solitude and already skilled at taking care of herself. It was not uncommon for her to prepare her own lunch and even dinner upon occasion. She often made sandwiches for her great-uncle Julio too, although sometimes needed his help opening a bag of potato chips or getting something from a high shelf.

After school, she would usually spend a couple of hours at Julio's house waiting for her mom or dad to get home from work. Not having children of his own, Julio was always happy to baby-sit and even referred to Margaret and her cousins in Florida as "his kids." He would often spend money on them— the little extra he had—but, possibly because he saw her so often, Margaret was his favorite and he took a particularly keen interest in how she was doing. And while she was very fond of him and lovingly called him "uncle," in truth she felt a greater affinity for her other, younger uncles. When she was told Uncle Julio had died, she did not seem extraordinarily upset.

Unable to find a baby-sitter the morning of Julio's viewing, Teresa and Mark reluctantly decided to bring her to the funeral parlor. It was not a large affair, a moderate gathering of friends and family, and they were careful to keep her several rooms from Julio's body so she wouldn't get upset. It went all right, nothing happened, just another day. Several weeks had passed since the event.

Margaret entered the kitchen, skating on her pajama feet across the linoleum. Teresa, recognizing the sound, turned from the stove.

"Hi, honey."

"Hi, Mom."

Margaret accepted a hug and kiss before climbing onto a chair at the table.

"I was just coming to get you," Teresa said. "You had a pretty big day yesterday, with Halloween and all. What would you like for breakfast?"

"Orange juice."

"That's all? You sure?"

"Yes."

"Okay, well, maybe you'll have something a little later."

"Okay."

It wasn't unusual for Margaret to skip breakfast and, even though she'd been sick with a flu the week before, Teresa was not particularly concerned. When it came to food, Margaret had a healthy appetite and was not at all a finicky or troubled eater. She could be persuaded to try almost anything without the usual scrunched-up faces and pouting. Without prodding, she recently had added fish and an array of vegetables to her diet, which pleased her parents very much. There was one food, though, that was far and away her favorite, and if you asked her what she'd like to have for lunch or dinner, the answer would always be the same: pizza.

The second day after Halloween, Margaret skipped breakfast again, except for a sip or two of juice. That night, despite the fact they had pizza for dinner, she said she wasn't hungry and just drank a little milk. By the following day, Margaret

15

was taking in only pure liquids; even the pulp in the orange juice was too substantive for her to swallow. And just that suddenly, the subject of food no longer held any interest for her. She didn't even want to look at food. Teresa and Mark were sure she was getting another cold or flu and, midweek, took her to their pediatrician.

He examined her thoroughly, weighed her, and could find nothing wrong. He told Teresa there was no need to be alarmed; Margaret was either getting over her last flu or coming down with something else.

Two days later, Margaret still had not eaten, so Teresa brought her back to the pediatrician. He had seen similar situations before and assured Teresa, in the absence of any other symptoms, it was likely just a phase. He said kids sometimes go through these things.

By the third visit, Margaret was beginning to lose weight, and the pediatrician was clearly perturbed, almost annoyed it would seem. "You know, if you don't start eating," he warned her, "you might have to go into the hospital. You don't want that, do you?"

She said no, but really didn't seem to care one way or the other. Her reaction, or lack thereof, increased Teresa's concern greatly. It struck her, as she watched the examination, that her daughter appeared lethargic and, of all things, depressed. Young children don't get depressed without severe provocation, do they? she wondered.

The following day, Margaret was supposed to attend a birthday party for one of her friends; she'd been looking forward to it for weeks and had mentioned it several times. Teresa hoped that in different surroundings, in the company of her playmates, her daughter's behavior might change. She asked the birthday girl's mother to keep an eye on Margaret to see if she ate anything. When Teresa returned later that afternoon, the birthday girl's mother informed her, to the best of her knowledge, Margaret hadn't eaten any of the lunch she served and later refused the cake and ice cream as well. Teresa shared her concerns with her husband that evening.

"I don't understand," Mark said. "If there's nothing wrong with her, why doesn't she eat something? Can't she just force herself?"

"I don't think so," was all Teresa could say.

Teresa contacted her brother, an art therapist, and he suggested Margaret come spend the weekend with him and his family, confident he could get her to eat. It seemed worth a try, so she and Mark made the long drive upstate and dropped Margaret off for the weekend. In the company of her cousins, she was taken to the movies, fast-food restaurants, ice cream parlors, pizza palaces galore, everything a kid would die for. She would not eat.

Upon hearing there was no change, the pediatrician insisted Teresa start bringing Margaret to see him every day. By the time he weighed her that Monday morning she had lost ten pounds. He sat her on the table, gave her a serious look, and said, "I'll give you another two pounds. But if you lose any more than that, we're going to have to put you in the hospital and tube-feed you. Do you understand?"

She nodded, but it was clear to Teresa his warning was having no effect. On the edge of panic, Teresa confided in a friend who, in turn, told her about a homeopath in Connecticut reputed to have astounding success with cases that had baffled traditional practitioners. Having no idea what homeopathy was, Teresa strapped Margaret into the car and headed north.

The homeopath talked with Margaret at length, videotaped her, studied her, and prescribed several solutions which he mixed in his office. Teresa saw to it that Margaret faithfully took the homeopathic remedies and continued to bring her to the pediatrician—but none of it was having any effect. In school, Margaret's lethargy was becoming increasingly evident; she could hardly hold her head up and frequently rested it on her desk. The teachers, who were informed of her condition, kept a watchful eye but never saw her so much as take a mouthful of food. After a brief consultation, the school psychologist referred Teresa and Mark to a local child psychiatrist.

Margaret had several sessions with the psychiatrist and, although he never actually said it, Teresa could tell he was of the opinion that the condition was psychosomatic. This seemed to be everyone's opinion, including Mark's. Confused and desperate, Teresa brought her daughter to a naturopath several towns away, but again with no positive results. It was mid-November and Margaret, who was always on the thin side, was beginning to look skeletal. Shuttling between the offices and ideologies of traditional and nontraditional practitioners did nothing to slow the shadow that crept ever closer. There was no rational explanation for what was happening, and there was no rational recourse.

2

A million miles away, I sat in my office staring at the phone, hoping it wouldn't ring, knowing it would. It had been almost a year since my experience with Amanda and, although I did not feel the slightest breeze, the winds of change were again about to sweep through my life and forever alter the landscape of my being. Amanda was the first child I'd worked with, a child for whom there was no hope beyond that which she instilled in others, and she was very much in my thoughts as the last of the season's leaves fell from the trees.

Actually, Matthew was the first child I had worked with, but since I was still a neophyte and didn't have a formal practice at the time, I never thought of him as a patient. My experience with him was one of those life events that occur out of the blue yet have such a profound and long-lasting effect that they become part of the fabric of your life. Matthew was like that for me; he changed my life. But it would take a decade and a child named Amanda before I fully realized it.

I was working at a leading financial institution when Matthew was born; his father was a key player in my department. It was there more than fifteen years ago that there first arose the issue of charity, which was why I was waiting for the phone to ring. Every year during the holidays, a company employee would ask for volunteers to work at the Westchester Homeless Shelter. I'd make my annual visit and do my share for the homeless, mostly because it felt good. But since I no longer worked for the financial institution, and had a business of my own, it was up to me to figure out what I could do for the shelter that holiday season. Thanksgiving dinner was my usual tour of duty and, having served so many times in the past, I knew exactly who to call and what to do. But I was hesitant. I knew the homeless were going to get fed that day whether I showed up or not. The truth was the shelter could handle this kind of event without me. I wasn't really needed. And besides, who was I to appear once a year and believe, in some way, this was a grand gesture?

Affected by these thoughts, the previous year I had made a point of talking to each person as I served them. I wanted to know who they were and how they had gotten there. Some were so young. After the last scoop of mashed potatoes was dished out, I took off my apron and approached a table where a group of four men were playing cards, using jelly beans for chips. I asked if I could join them, and they said no. I asked if I could watch, and they just grumbled.

Three of the men appeared to be middle-aged, with hair peppered with gray, while the fourth was noticeably younger. One of the three wore a bright red knitted cap that seemed incongruent with his soggy, depressed mood and drab, dirty shirt. I wondered if he wanted to be noticed or just blend into the woodwork. He sent both messages simultaneously.

"Where did you get your hat?" I asked.

"Where da ya think," he grumbled, "Bloomingdale's?"

They all laughed and returned their attention to the game. The man in the red cap had a strong jaw and soft, hooded eyes; he seemed to be the unofficial leader. Whenever he spoke, the rest of the group responded as though they had just been given permission to join in—but they always waited for him to speak first. Now he was quiet, focused on something unseen, internal, or maybe he was just concentrating on his cards. There was no way to know, he never lifted his eyes from his hand. I waited for an opening that never came and finally, with trepidation, inserted myself into their silence. I turned to the man in the red cap, lightly touched his shoulder, and asked the question I had been wondering about from the start, "What happened? How did you get here?" For a moment he sat motionless and then laid his cards down, grabbing everyone's attention. "Exactly how much do you want to know and how much time have you got?" he said, looking me square in the eye. Twenty minutes later, the men were tripping over one another, anxious to be heard by someone outside their circle. It occurred to me, that in places like the shelter where people are often told what to do, where to go, where to find work, and where to sleep, they are rarely valued as unique individuals.

While all their stories were fascinating, the man in the red cap had by far the most to say. As I listened, he seemed to come to life, his posture and attitude lifted, and I was certain it was the conversation and not the meal that had energized him so. The other men would periodically join in with anecdotes from their life stories, and I found myself completely engrossed, drawn into their lives; I was young and naive, and honestly had no idea how a person became homeless. As the evening went on, the more I leaned into their lives, the more they leaned into mine.

The youngest of the four men had been sitting next to me through most of the conversation. His hair was free of gray, his eyes bloodshot but large and round with a hint of desire, lingering like an ember just before it flares into a flame. His anxiety was obvious; he could not sit still, and his eyes darted from face to face. At one point, as his agitation grew increasingly disturbing to me, I instinctively laid my hand on the back of his. It was an affectionate but casual gesture on my part, and I was unprepared for his response. He froze, literally stopped mid-sentence, and stared at our hands. The tension was permeable, and he lowered his head before speaking. "I can't remember ever being touched in kindness by an adult woman—not once in my entire life."

The pain escaped through his eyes and, unable to hide my sadness, I was grateful when the other men joined in with tears of their own. We remained at that table until well after midnight when we were asked to leave. A rather large group of men followed me into the parking lot, and I realized it was to ensure I made it to my car safely. In the chilly night air, I hugged each and every one of them before driving away with the knowledge I had been given as much and more than I had come to give. Although I never knew their names, they had revealed themselves and their mark was on me, indelible, just like Matthew.

Something ignited in my soul that night at the homeless shelter that yearned to be expressed more than once a year, without reason, without the need of a specific holiday or a man in a red hat. And so a year later, sitting in my office, an idea began to take shape. I did not recognize the power of the thought when it first arose and, if I had, I'm not certain I would have pursued it. In fact, if I had recognized what this thought actually was, I'm quite sure I'd have scared myself right out of it. Staring at the phone on my desk, I prayed out loud so I'd be sure to hear myself, *I will give my services at no charge to the next person who calls—whoever it is, for however long I'm needed, whatever the reason. So be it.*

I had no idea to whom I was committing, what they'd want, or even if I could help in any way. In fact, the more I thought about it, the worse an idea it seemed, and I soon had a different message for the universe: *I don't have to go through with this, do I? No one would know if I changed my mind—the phone hasn't rung yet. Maybe volunteering for the homeless shelter isn't such a bad idea after all. Maybe the phone won't ring.*

But it did ring. An impossibly short fifteen minutes later, unable to recall another prayer so quickly answered, I reluctantly picked up the receiver on the third ring, just ahead of the answering machine.

"This is Roseanne."

"Hi, Roseanne, it's Teresa Prentiss. Do you remember me?"

"Teresa! Of course I remember you. How have you been?"

I knew Teresa from the financial institution where we worked together years earlier. Although we hadn't been close friends, and never socialized outside of the office, I knew her well enough to know she was smart, organized, never got riled, and was a pleasure to work with. Hearing her voice was a great relief, although I was somewhat curious as to how she got my office number; we hadn't seen each other or even spoken since I'd left the company.

"Are you still working in finance?" I asked

"Yes. In fact, I'm still with the same company."

"That's terrific. I bet a lot has changed."

"You'd barely recognize the place."

"Yeah, that's how it is with me, too."

We went on like this for several minutes. But I knew this was not a casual how-have-you-been; this was *the* phone call and, while glad to catch up on the past, I anxiously waited through the small talk.

"Claudia's still with the company," she said.

"Oh yeah? How's she doing?"

"She's doing fine. Really, very well."

"Be sure to give her my regards."

"I will. Actually, she was the one who suggested I call you."

Here we were.

"Concerning what, Teresa?"

"Well, it's about my daughter, Margaret."

Oh no. "How old is she?"

"She's only six."

No, no, no.

"And the doctors . . ."

I can't do this again.

" . . . say she's in a great deal of trouble."

I can't. I won't.

"They say she could die."

Please, dear God, not another sick little girl, not another Amanda.

The conversation just seemed to hang there a moment. Hoping I didn't sound the way I felt, I finally said, "Tell me the details."

"Well, we've seen doctors and psychiatrists, and none of them have any idea what's going on with Margaret. She can't seem to bring herself to eat. She starts to gag every time she tries. We've had all the medical work done, everything science has to offer, but no one can figure out the cause. It's been weeks since she's had any solid food, and she's starting to get pretty thin. They say the problem may have something to do with the peristalsis in her digestive tract." (Peristalsis is the natural, rhythmic contraction of the muscles that moves food through the esophagus, stomach, and intestines.)

"It's affecting the whole family, and we have no idea what to do about it. We've tried absolutely everything we could think of, but she just can't eat . . . or won't. She's only a few pounds away from mandatory hospitalization and intravenous feeding. They tell us it's the only way to save her from going into a coma. But they also say if it gets to that point . . ."

I could hear her start to cry on the other end of the line and tried my best to comfort her. Despite the desperation of the situation, I still wondered what would motivate such a down-to-earth person to call me, a practitioner so outside of the mainstream—and then I remembered something that happened when we were working together.

Teresa was pregnant with her second child (Margaret being the first) and I happened to walk past her desk to drop something off down the hall. For whatever reason, at the time she had not told anyone of the pregnancy. Nonetheless, I showered her with best wishes and congratulations and asked when she was due. She blanched and didn't respond. Noticing her discomfort, I quickly retreated to my office, feeling thoroughly the villain although unsure what exactly I had done; I hoped her pregnancy was a joyous occasion and I hadn't put my foot in my mouth in some way.

A short while later, she entered my office and closed the door behind her. She was a little agitated but mostly inquisitive, certain a confidence had been breached. When she asked how I knew about the pregnancy, I told her how sorry I was for being indiscreet. "I wasn't thinking," I explained, "I just blurted it out."

"But how did you know about it?"

"I just did. Sometimes things just pop into my head and then out of my mouth."

There's no explaining when your mouth knows the answer before your brain does. It's a trait that, until I learned to control it, often got me into trouble. As a child I was always telling my mother when people were lying, being secretive, or insensitive. These outbursts tended to be something of an embarrassment as I rarely waited for privacy before speaking up. And there I was doing it again, opening my big mouth about Teresa's pregnancy. To the best of my recollection, this was the only incident that might have given her any faith in me. It didn't seem like enough but, at the same time, it didn't really matter.

"When can you come in?" I asked.
"As soon as you can see us."

3

There is nothing extraordinary about my office. It's the kind of place you drive by all the time and never notice. The setting is relatively rural and unimpressive—no spectacular views, no interesting architecture. Just a plain, gray ranch house that has been converted into commercial space.

My office is on the ground floor. It has pretty good light and three entrances—although I rarely use the back door since the lock broke and became difficult to deal with. I recently had the room repainted and, although I neglected to have the lock fixed, the walls are now light pink, the windows and doors trimmed in white. The slightest smell of paint still lingers.

I share a waiting room with the real estate business that's upstairs and I often hear their comings and goings. Some days they are quite busy. They have a large sign near the road which makes it less likely one of my clients will miss the turn, even if lost in some internal dialogue. I don't have a sign or even a shingle—just a door and one room. I don't advertise or have a brochure. I tell those who inquire that, in my work, I use all my life experience and formal training, all my degrees, all the modalities and resources from my past and present, all my insights and gut reactions—all my everything.

The office is largely undecorated except for the things people give me. Grouped together on the longest exterior wall are my diplomas—some traditional, some not. Some inexplicable. One is a drawing of the Archangel Hanael, whose job is to watch over all the mothers in the world and protect them from harm, guarding the people we assume are guarding us. Next to Hanael is a photograph of my nephew; he's about four years old in the picture and thoroughly full of himself. Every time I look at his lovable, impish little face, I fully expect him to stick his tongue out at me. Of all the things here, I love this picture the most.

At the far end of the room is a massage table, a gift, retrieved from a friend's basement. It's made of warm old oak with folding legs and supports held in place by tarnished wing nuts. It's all very solid and slightly wobbly at the same time. A six-year-old would not be tall enough to see the very top of the table, but would likely notice the side of the navy blue padding that covers the top. No, there is nothing extraordinary about my office, and visitors are often disappointed by its ordinariness; frankly, so was I when I first rented it. But it is conveniently located, has a private entrance, its own temperature control, and my patients, be they four or sixty-four, can make plenty of noise if they need to. It serves its purpose.

I had to adjust my schedule considerably to accommodate Teresa and did so despite the inner doubts I still harbored. My experience with Amanda, the memory of which was never distant, helped me to develop a higher degree of self-trust, but it would be stretching the point to describe it as confidence. A few days after we spoke on the phone, I greeted Teresa in the waiting area. She looked much as I remembered with soft features, big blue eyes, and a slight natural blush to her cheeks. She was not heavy or overweight but there was a softness about her. She was of medium height with short brown hair and tender, delicate skin—her emotions finding their home not far from its surface. I was warmed by her energy as I hugged her.

Margaret had short blond hair and many of her mother's features. She was extremely well behaved. She entered the office holding her mother's hand, careful not to touch anything, very grown-up but at the same time thoroughly sweet and tender. The pink and purple parka she wore over her baggy overalls did not hide how exceptionally thin she was, and yet it was neither her weight nor her fatigue that I found most disturbing: it was the dark circles under her eyes. Although logically attributed to malnutrition, there was something else about them, something I recognized.

I said "Hi," and Margaret smiled shyly and then looked away.

She and Teresa sat down on one of the couches and I sat across from them. It seemed significant that Margaret didn't instinctually pick up the teddy bear lying next to her, satisfied to sit quietly until otherwise instructed. It was impossible to know how this all appeared to her, but I periodically followed her eyes as she looked around the room. Assuming she had a child's clarity about what she saw, I felt foolishly self-conscious; the office was far from a typical doctor's office and I wasn't wearing a white coat. I was wearing what I always wore to work: comfortable, casual, washable clothes—no silk, no suits, nothing that might need dry cleaning or special care. (This way, if someone throws up on me, cries on my shoulder, or wipes a nose on my sleeve, I'm not distracted by having something I like ruined.)

As I followed Margaret's eyes around the room, across and occasionally through me, even as I spoke with her mother, I was able to gather some sense of who she was. I already felt an unspoken connection to this child and if I understood nothing else, I knew the work would evolve from the depths of that connection. My slight hope that she was pleased by what she saw was, in itself, an insight.

Although I had a sense of Margaret herself, I didn't have any immediate insights about her condition. I still hoped there was some obvious physical cause for her inability to eat despite the knowledge that, if this had been the case, the doctors would surely have discovered it. Teresa handed me the intake form and I began to look it over. It basically repeated, in greater depth, what she had already told me on the phone. Under *reason for visit*, it simply read, "not eating." As it was, the best Margaret could do was to take the smallest sip of tea, broth, or water—less than an ounce—and then only rarely. The last time Teresa could recall her daughter eating any solid food was more than a month before their visit, on October 31, Halloween.

Teresa wrote out a chronological list of events leading up to that last meal. On October 26, Margaret had gotten sick with the symptoms typical of a flu virus and ate very little throughout the illness. The fever subsided, but her ability to swallow and hold down food continued to deteriorate and by the day after Halloween she was not eating at all. The doctors felt the bout with the virus was unrelated to her eating disorder.

Going back farther, she wrote, that on October 4, Margaret's great-uncle Julio quite suddenly and unexpectedly collapsed and died. He had been ill for six years, Margaret's entire life. Somehow this seemed wildly important to me. It stood out on the paper as if it were written in large bold type. I was already certain Margaret wasn't a rebellious child refusing to eat, belligerently clamping her jaw shut, or anything like that. There was an absolute and total willingness within this child to please others, and she would have unquestionably eaten if she could have. This was not an act of rebellion, it was an act of love.

"Tell me, Teresa, were Margaret and her great-uncle close? I mean, did they see a lot of each other? Did he live far away?"

"Oh no. They were very, very close. He lived down the street in his own house. In fact, he would baby-sit Margaret when she'd come home from school. My husband and I usually get home an hour or two after Margaret's bus drops her off. So, we were lucky Julio was there."

I was increasingly certain that the timing of Uncle Julio's death was more than mere coincidence. "Do you know what their relationship was like?" I asked.

"Well, Julio had been sick for several years, so I think they did quiet things like playing cards and board games."

"So, she was with him basically every day of her recent life?"

"Yes."

"And now her after-school routine is different."

"Yes, that's right."

"If it's okay with you, Teresa, I'd like to get started with Margaret."

She said it was, and I moved to the other couch and sat down next to Margaret. I asked her if she wanted to play with Bear and she responded, "Sure." Although I could tell she didn't care one way or the other, she dutifully picked up the white bear, reinforcing my assessment that her essential predilection was to please. In attempting to work with her, this was problematic since her outer behavior, unconsciously motivated, was designed to hide her true nature and gut-level reactions. She presented the unflappable picture of a "good girl."

I asked Margaret to hold Bear and mimic my every motion. She held him weakly and carefully tried to accommodate me. It was an awkward process; she was all too anxious to follow my instructions, which served to mask her genuine reactions. So easy she was hard. At one point, Bear slipped out of her hands, falling to the floor, and I instinctually reached out to hold her. "It's okay, just leave him there," I said, startled by what I felt. It wasn't the physical feeling of her emaciated body that was so unsettling, but a peculiar sensation that seemed to emanate from her. It was like reaching into a paper bag and touching something unexpected, something that didn't belong there, something chilling. Margaret didn't flinch or give any outward sign of discomfort; she simply remained cooperative.

"Would it be okay if I touched your tummy?"

She said yes, but I could feel her tense up and it was obvious she didn't want me to come anywhere near her abdomen. I brought my hand no closer than a foot from her midsection when she winced and actually gasped for air. It was as though I had squeezed her stomach so hard she couldn't breathe. I backed off and told her I had come close enough and didn't really need to touch her. She appeared greatly relieved to hear this.

I asked if she'd like to take a closer look at the pictures on the wall and, when she said yes, I led her across the room and pointed out a few of my favorites. I returned and sat down next to Teresa. "I know you don't understand what's going on and probably have a lot of questions. You can ask me anything you want."

Teresa just kept nodding at me.

"What I want to do is investigate the deeper issues at the heart of why this is happening to Margaret," I said. "Rather than have her in a sitting position, which scrunches the energy at the waist, I might need her to lie down on the massage table."

"Why?" Teresa asked.

"So that I can see what her energy is doing. It's easier for me when she's lying down."

"Do whatever you need to do, Roseanne."

I wanted to include Teresa as much as possible and keep her informed, but I was also giving Margaret a chance to disengage from the "adults" and not be the center of attention for a moment. When I was sure Margaret was completely unaware of my actions, I whispered to Teresa, "I want to show you something. I'm going to touch Margaret's stomach with only my energy and not my physical hand. Imagine my arm is six feet longer than it actually is; two feet of physical arm and six feet of energy, like the beam of a flashlight. Then consider for a moment that Margaret is as sensitive to that energy as she is to my physical hand."

Teresa just looked at me, probably thinking this was some sort of New Age foolishness on my part. Outwardly, however, she was completely and appropriately polite.

"Watch this," I said.

Margaret was about eight feet away studying the pictures on the wall. Something in one of the photos had captured her attention. Very subtly, I moved my hand from my lap, extended it ever so slightly, then held it absolutely still. Slowly I began to regulate my energy so that it flowed from my hand towards Margaret's tummy, arcing across the room until it gently touched her midriff, right below her rib cage. Although my physical hand was still a full seven feet away, she had a pronounced reaction and became visibly uncomfortable almost to the point of gagging. Teresa's eyes nearly popped out of her head.

"I know all this must seem a little odd but, as you can see, your daughter is extremely sensitive and there is something going on in the region of her solar plexus. I don't know what it's all about but I'd like to find out."

"I would deeply appreciate anything you can do to help her."

"I don't know if I can help her, Teresa, but I'll try. You're welcome to stay and watch, but I'd prefer you didn't say anything while the work is in progress—unless, of course, you should want me to stop for some reason. You can ask me all the questions you want after I'm done."

"Just go ahead and do what you can for her," she said. "I don't need to understand, and you don't have to explain."

For her own reasons, Teresa chose not to remain for the session and retreated to the waiting room. Whatever made her comfortable was fine with me, although this wasn't my standard operating procedure. "There's a window in the office door so you can watch what's happening. Or, if you change your mind, just come back in."

"No, that's okay. Come get me when you're done."

The moment Teresa left the room, Margaret's energy underwent a noticeable change. While in her mother's company she was deeply worried, fully aware of the strain her illness was putting on her family, her mother in particular. Alone with me, she began to relax a little bit.

I helped her onto the table and had her lay on her back. She was remarkably trusting. "This is a massage table you're lying on," I said. "Have you ever had a massage?"

She giggled and said, "No. Are you going to give me a massage?"

"No, not really, but I am going to play with the energy that surrounds your body, inside and out." I asked if I could hold her hand and she quickly responded in the affirmative. "Are you by any chance ticklish?"

"Yes," she giggled.

"Well, don't worry. I'm not going to tickle you, but I would like to hold your feet just like I'm holding your hand. Is it okay if I do that?"

"Uh-huh."

"Good. I'll be very careful."

I gently cupped the bottom of her feet, my thumbs on her soles, considered the reflex point of the solar plexus, my fingers wrapped around her toes. Margaret giggled nervously and I smiled back at her. Barely touching her, featherlike, I began running energy through her system, looking to see if it was having an effect or disturbing her in anyway. This is the first step in a process created by Rosayln Bruyere called a "chelation," which is based on the concept that energy flows from the greater amount to the lesser amount; it's a natural, physical phenomenon.[1] In this instance, I represented the "greater" energy source not solely because I was an adult, but also because Margaret was totally depleted and the energy seemed to be draining out of her when it should have been coming in as a source of nourishment. In addition, being six years old, Margaret's energy body, just like her physical body, had not yet fully developed, leaving her vulnerable and extremely sensitive.[2]

Allowing the energy to flow, acting solely as a conduit, not orchestrating anything, I watched as her field began to clear.

Putting energy into her system had an inherent effect: the energy went exactly where it was needed and did exactly what it needed to do—like water taking the shape of its container. It also revealed the location of anomalies, that is to say, places where Margaret's energy was blocked.

I asked Margaret to close her eyes. "Imagine," I whispered, "that it hasn't rained for many, many years and everything is dry and dusty. Even the river is dry and full of litter, leaves, and twigs. Then one day it begins to rain, and it rains and rains and rains, and the river fills up with water and starts to flow again. As the water rushes downstream, it picks up the old candy wrappers and twigs and sweeps them out to sea, cleaning and revitalizing the river, actually bringing it back to life. That's kind of what's happening with you, Margaret. As I touch each of your legs, arms, and energy centers, you fill up with energy, just like the river filled up with water. And just like the water helped the river, the energy will help to clear away your worries and woes, and maybe even some of your aches and pains too. But you're only six, so you don't have any of those, do you?"

She giggled a little, mostly for my sake. I laughed too, mostly for hers. The anomaly in her field was daunting, more like a boulder that had fallen into the river than a piece of litter. Obviously an anomaly of this size could not so easily be cleared away.

I began moving up Margaret's body, using my fingertips to gently touch each of her tiny joints—ankles, knees, hips—informing her of my every move before I made it. I explained that my hands were like garden hoses with energy flowing through them instead of water, and that she, like a thirsty flower, drank that energy right up. I noticed that the more information I gave her, the more relaxed she became. I marveled at what an exceptionally cerebral child she was, finding safety in the mental realms although she had no idea what I was talking about. This was where her being a six-year-old was extremely helpful; she never attempted to rationalize this new material. She, more or less, just tried to have fun with it, not concerned whether it was fact or fantasy. It was probably no less comprehensible than the information the doctors had shared concerning her physiology.

She appeared interested and increasingly more at ease as we proceeded, but when I put both my hands on her hips something inside me suddenly began to ache for her. She did not display any outward sign of worry or fear, and I could tell she didn't know what was going on and questioning her would be pointless. But it was clear she didn't want me to bring my hands any closer to her midsection and I promised I wouldn't, even energetically, without her permission.

It was important to keep Margaret informed of everything I was doing; that was how she felt safe. I told her that there were invisible vortexes emanating from each of us, little spinning wheels that fed energy into our bodies called chakras. I explained that she, like everyone else, had seven of them.

"The first chakra is the lowest one on your body and it's red. The second," I said as I placed my hand below my belly button, "is here, and it's orange. The third one is just below your ribs and it's bright yellow. The fourth is right here." I placed my hand between my breasts and sighed so she got the idea. "This is called the heart chakra and it's green, the same color as grass."

She frowned and said, "I thought hearts were red."

"Like valentines?"

"Yes."

"Well, when you're in love, they sort of are."

She seemed to like that.

"The throat chakra is the fifth one and right now yours is blue," I continued. "There's also a chakra in the middle of your forehead and it's the color of the sky at night. And finally, at the top of your head is your seventh chakra, and it's usually white."

The more I went on, the bigger her eyes got.

"I don't see anything," she whispered.

"Try closing your eyes," I said. "Sometimes that works better."

The look on Margaret's face told me she had absolutely no idea what I was talking about, but she kept her attention fixed on my every move, watching me, examining me, in fact. I didn't say there was anything wrong with any of her chakras; I simply pointed out their location and said it was her job to tell me how they felt. Wanting so very much to please but not knowing how, she tensed up and worried about giving "incorrect" answers to my queries. Her inability to discern what "correct" was made pleasing impossible and, after a while, actually had a calming effect on her.

Our conversation about chakras and energy fields gave us the framework in which to play a game concerning her abdominal region—a game in which she, better than I, understood the rules.

"Can I come this close?" I said, my hand five or six feet from her stomach.

She said yes and I moved my hand a little closer.

"How about if I come this close?" I asked.

"Okay."

"And this close?"

"It's okay."

"Good," I said. "You're doing really well. I'm going to bring my hand just a little bit closer, all right?"

She fought off a nervous giggle and nodded yes.

This went on until my hand was about six inches from her stomach.

"Can I come a little closer?"

Although she again said yes, she was gritting her teeth and, it was obvious, her unspoken answer was "absolutely not."

"I don't want you to say it's okay unless you really mean it. If you don't want me to come any closer, then I won't. I promise."

This threw her into something of a quandary. She was increasingly aware of the contradiction between her own words and her spontaneous physical reactions, her conscious mind saying yes, her body saying no.

"I'm not going to do anything to surprise you but I'd like to move my hand just one inch closer. Just one inch. Would that be okay?"

She nodded yes but fear escaped through her big blue eyes, now wide with worry.

"You'd rather I didn't do this, right, Margaret?"

"No, it's okay."

"Because if it's not okay, I won't move my hand closer until it is."

"It's okay, I want you to," she said.

"All right, then," I said, "but I want you to tell me if you don't like it, or if it hurts, or if you want me to stop."

I continued to work an inch at a time, always allowing her to make the decision. And although I knew she'd rather I didn't have my hand there at all, this process was slowly teaching her the difference between invasion and permission. Margaret fully believed it was her job to please and readily allowed authority figures to do things to her she'd rather not have done. She did not easily acknowledge or exercise her right to say "no," but there came a moment when her body began to scream it despite the fact her head was nervously nodding "yes." It was then I decided the game should end and that we should work/play in a more general, less localized, manner.

Her overly compliant nature and tendency to minimize her emotional reactions convinced me that there was, at least, a strong possibility that some secret trauma had occurred. I did not want to do anything to add to that trauma but, at the same time, I urgently needed to discover the truth. Eventually, I was going to have to get into this region to find and clear whatever was causing this tremendous resistance. But what exactly was going to be uncovered, cleared, or released?

And what effect would this process have? The intangibles were looming ever greater than the tangibles, but for the moment it was essential that I respect Margaret's boundaries . . . which were practically nonexistent.

The session was nearing its conclusion, so I moved my hands to her other chakras and asked her to close her eyes and tell me what she saw. I wasn't concerned whether she saw anything or not, I was just trying to engage her, to deepen our repartee, to demystify the experience. At first she was unable to respond, but after a while she shyly began to question me about the energy in and around her body.

"Are all my chakras spinning?" she whispered.

"Yes, just like pinwheels."

"Are they pretty?"

"Yes, of course, beautiful. Why?"

"Because I want to know."

She was playing along but it was easy to see she didn't really buy any of it. I continued to work on her chakras, moving my hands over her body, careful not to come too close. I asked what she thought of the proceedings and, not wanting to say anything that wasn't nice or polite, she self-consciously replied, "I don't know."

"I can tell you think this is all pretty silly, don't you?"

"Yes."

"And it must seem a little strange; me making funny noises and funny faces and waving my hands in the air, right?"

"Yes."

"Well, I'm a very silly person sometimes."

She broke up into laughter upon hearing this. I thought that it seemed the perfect moment to mention what I had been wondering from the start.

"Your mom told me that your Uncle Julio died recently. Do you miss him?"

She didn't tense up or get emotional in any way but simply said, "Yes."

"Tell me about him and what you did together." I later

37

found out the psychiatrists had already gone down this road and asked many of the same questions—which explained Margaret's complacency in answering. I was considerably more uneasy about it then she was.

"So, tell me, what did the two of you do?"

"We played cards."

"I know, but you must have done more than just that. I mean, you would come home from school and then what?"

"We'd play cards."

"How about before that, when you would first arrive at his house. What would you guys do?"

"Nothing."

I tried to keep things in the "silly" world and in a funny voice said, "You must have done something—like talk or laugh or breathe, for goodness sake!?"

She started laughing again, which got me going as well. Between the giggles, I insisted she tell me every single little thing that happened.

She said, "Well, the first thing I'd do is take off my coat."

"And what did you do with it?"

"I hung it up."

"And then what?"

"Well, usually, Uncle Julio wanted me to get him something."

"Like what?"

"I would get Uncle Julio something to drink."

"That was very nice of you. What else did you do?"

"We'd play cards together."

"And if he got hungry while you were playing?"

"I would go make him something to eat—a sandwich or crackers or something."

"Anything else?"

"Well, not really."

"Are you sure?"

"Well, Uncle Julio was tired a lot so I'd get things for him when he asked me to."

"You did? Well, it sounds like you're very grown up."

I couldn't help but notice that here was a man who was supposed to be baby-sitting, taking care of a young child, but the very first thing she said about him, translated into adult language, was that she was taking care of him. It was not surprising; after all, she took care of her mother by letting her leave the room and she tried to take care of me by giving the right answers to my questions—careful not to say anything that wasn't nice. There was little doubt this also characterized the relationship with her great-uncle. It was a perfect fit; a chronically ill, needy adult and a child anxious to please. She was, in a sense, his substitute spouse.

"Was there anybody else there?"

"No, just Uncle Julio and me."

Concerned this whole subject was beginning to make Margaret uneasy, I reached for her in an attempt at a small hug. Once again I experienced an extremely peculiar feeling, like someone was watching us. "You know the games we've been playing, describing the spinning colors and things?"

"Yes."

"Well, I'd like to play another game. Okay?"

"Okay."

"Do you ever still talk to Uncle Julio?"

"No." She thought I was being silly again.

"Because you can still talk to people although they're gone."

"No, that's silly. I can't talk to someone who's not here."

"Well, you remember him, don't you?"

"Yes."

"And you can remember how you felt about him."

"Yes."

"How did you feel about him?"

"I loved him."

"You did?"

"Yes, I loved Uncle Julio and I still do."

"Good. Hey, I've got an idea. Why don't we see if Uncle

Julio can help you with this problem you've been having. You know, people we love are always happy to help us."

This seemed plausible to her and she said, "Okay."

"Then what I'd like you to do is, between now and the next time I see you, ask Uncle Julio if he'll help you eat. And do it three times a day, all right?"

"All right."

"Great. Let's try it now. Go ahead, ask Uncle Julio to help you eat and say it out loud for practice."

The seconds passed but she remained silent.

"Why won't you say it?"

"Because it's too silly."

"Try."

Margaret rolled her eyes but remained mute.

"Well, how about this, can you say it in your head? You know, silently, so no one can hear but you and Uncle Julio?"

Exasperated, she reluctantly sighed, "Okaayyyy."

"Good, then do it that way."

She looked away and, I hoped, internally made the effort.

"Do you think he heard you? Do you think it worked?"

She was just going through the motions when she nodded, but I wanted, probably needed, to believe we were making some sort of tangible progress. "How do you feel? Do you think you can eat?" I clumsily asked.

With the slightest motion of her head, she said yes.

Really? Could it be this easy?

I had brought a simple lunch to the office that day which consisted of cheese, fruit, and bread. I ripped the tiniest piece of crust from the bread and handed it to her. "Here," I said as casually as I could, "let's share."

She took it and held it for a moment before lifting it to her lips. I immediately knew this was causing her more pain than good; struggling, trying hard as she could, there was no way she could put it in her mouth, let alone eat it. I said, "Honey, you don't have to. We have lots of time."

I knew my hope for instant magic, divine intervention on demand, was wishful thinking but I couldn't help myself. I so wanted to tell Teresa, "Go home and fix dinner for your lovely daughter; there's nothing more to worry about." As it was, we hadn't made a shred of progress and now, here I was, solidly in love with this wonderful little girl who was gradually starving to death.

I took a business card from my desk and handed it to Margaret. "You know, you can call me if you want. See, here's my name and number. You don't have to wait for your mom or anything, you can just call me yourself." She held the card in her tiny hands and looked at it. "Now that you're talking to Uncle Julio—although he's in Heaven and not in the room with you—you never know, you might get the urge to talk to me, too. I know some of what we said sounded silly, but silly's pretty good sometimes. So if you ever want to talk about anything at all, you'll call, right?"

She said yes to everything, but I knew she didn't really mean it. It occurred to me I should be more direct and, with just a few minutes left in the session, I made another effort to connect with her.

"How do you feel about not being able to eat?" I gently asked. She didn't know what to say, so I continued, "You understand that you're here because your mom's worried about you not eating?"

"Yes."

"Do you want to eat?"

"Yes."

"Do you know why you can't eat?" I was asking questions I already knew the answers to and she was getting more upset as I went on.

"No," she said.

"You want to eat but you just can't, is that right?"

She nodded, head down, tears slowly filling her blue eyes, her lower lip stiff.

"And you don't know why any of this is happening, do you?"

She shook her head and it was obvious how deeply affected she was, how intense her desire to be "well," to be "normal," to please. Not wanting to leave things on this note, hoping to lighten the mood a bit, I asked what, at the time, seemed like the most innocent, natural question in the world—the question children are asked over and over again at this time of year.

"You know Santa will be coming soon?"

"Yes, yes. I do."

"And you know what that means?"

"What?"

"Presents, of course. Christmas presents. So, what do you want for Christmas?"

She got very still and looked me square in the eye and said, "I don't want anything."

"There must be something you want . . . a game, a doll? You must want something?"

After a pause, in a voice barely audible, she finally said, "I want to be able to eat. I just want to be able to eat Christmas dinner with my family."

Her lower lip was trembling now, her jaw tightly set as she hugged herself, arms across her belly protecting the tender, vulnerable place. Her doll-like hands curled up into little clenched fists and she said, "I just want to be able to eat. That's all!"

With that, she could hold it in no longer and collapsed onto my lap, crying fully and deeply. "I just want to be able to eat, I just want to eat," she sobbed.

I held her in helpless silence for several minutes. Then she blew her nose, put on her coat, and, as if nothing much had occurred, headed for the waiting room. Teresa stood as we entered.

"Would you mind if I spoke with your mother alone for a minute?"

Margaret accepted the children's magazine I offered her and Teresa and I returned to the office. I questioned her about Uncle Julio, wanting to know exactly what the relationship was, trying to make sure I had every aspect of the story correct. She repeated what Margaret had already told me; they saw each other every day, watched TV, played cards.

"You mentioned he was chronically ill. Is it possible Margaret could have fetched for him? A run-and-fetch type of thing?"

"Yes, she'd get him a sandwich or a drink and do basic chores for him."

"I don't want to alarm you, Teresa. But somehow I just don't feel like the relationship was as it should be." I deliberately avoided using the word "abusive." I certainly didn't know what had happened and had no desire to throw Teresa any deeper into turmoil.

This line of inquiry was not new to her, but Teresa's faltering voice betrayed an underlying doubt. "The psychiatrists explored this same area and their determination was that she wasn't abused." Teary-eyed, she asked, "Do you think she was?"

"I don't know, Teresa. I really don't know." Our eyes locked and I continued. "I just know the relationship with Julio was not what I would call normal. There seems to have been an inversion of roles that, to me, doesn't feel quite right. Whether something happened beyond this, I can't tell. But there's enough there to make me want to look further. Can you come back? I'd like to see Margaret again, in less than a week if possible."

We scheduled an appointment for December sixteenth and I deliberately picked up the pace, not wanting to address the other question I saw in her eyes. It was the same one I'd seen in the eyes of Amanda's mother the year before: *Can you save my baby?*

"Before I forget, how much do you charge?" she asked. "I want to write out a check."

"There's no charge."

"That's very kind of you, Roseanne, but I absolutely insist on paying you."

I tried to explain how her call was the answer to my prayer and not the other way around, but she, of course, didn't believe one word of it.

"I just wouldn't feel right about not paying."

"Believe me, Teresa, the decision about not excepting a fee was made before I even knew it was you who was calling. This is for my benefit, a gift to myself."

She was not easily dissuaded and I struggled to think of something that might convince her. "Do you remember when we worked together, how a bunch of us used to volunteer to work at the homeless shelter during the holidays?"

She reluctantly nodded.

"Well, I no longer work at the shelter. Instead, I randomly choose one phone call during the holidays and offer my services without charge."

"That's very sweet of you, Roseanne, but I really . . ."

"I mean it, Teresa, no matter what you say or do, my mind is made up. I'm not taking your money. So let's talk about something else. I'd like to know how you're holding up under this enormous strain."

She sighed and let the issue pass. "I guess I'm pretty beat up. It hasn't been easy trying to deal with this." She paused to collect herself. "It's particularly tough on my husband, there being no diagnosis, no reason for Margaret's behavior. He can't understand why she just won't eat, and I don't know what to tell him."

"Tell him Margaret's not doing this on purpose. It's really important he understands that. And tell him he's welcome to come here with you if he wants. I'd be happy to talk to him."

"Thanks. We're both afraid she's going to end up in the hospital. The doctors said even if they use a stomach tube and feed her intravenously it would only serve to slow down the process but not stop it. Eventually her muscles would atrophy and she'd fall into a coma."

I still couldn't believe I was hearing this; it was Amanda all over again. "Teresa, I want to tell you, so you're not disappointed, not to expect any change in Margaret's behavior this week. She's under a great deal of stress so, if I might suggest, don't try to make her eat, it just adds to her anxiety. She wants to eat, she wants to please you, and will if she can. I'd love for there to be a turnabout in her condition and I'll be praying for one, but please don't get your hopes up or look for any immediate improvement." I'm not sure if I said this for Teresa's sake or my own.

"I understand," she replied, nodding as she spoke, her eyes telling a different story.

"Please call me if there's any change, any change whatsoever," I went on. "In fact, if you don't mind, I might call you."

"Of course. Call any time."

"Great. Now what I'd like you to do tonight is give her something easy to digest just in case she can eat. Something like mashed potatoes or pastina, something easy. No steak."

She smiled at the absurdity of this last comment, and the first session was over. I saw them to the door and slowly closed it behind them. All alone, I fell apart. Despite the fact that I had vivid images of the dynamics of the case—I even had an idea of what to do—it was all smoke in the wind. All I knew for sure was that God had answered my prayer with another precious little girl who was in the process of dying.

4

I ate a sparse dinner that night, then sat around wondering how I could have gotten myself into a situation like this again.

Of course, this time I was here by choice: in an effort to find fulfillment, I had chosen to pray. That prayer had not led me into peace and tranquillity, self-contentment, or grace, but into the unknown where there were no answers, only more questions.

Actually, I was not surprised when Teresa expressed no interest in the nature of my work with Margaret, the hows and whys. She did not want explanations or education; she wanted a well baby, a healthy little girl, a normal child. I had done the best I could, what I was trained to do. I applied all the techniques I'd studied and practiced over the years. I worked with Margaret in ways that not only included but transcended traditional modalities. I tried everything: I told her stories, held her hand, looked into her eyes, searched my soul. I even incorporated humor. I was willing to consider anything, but nothing seemed to be enough. Margaret needed more and I felt empty.

I wanted to hold her, physically and spiritually. I wanted to bring her through this, take away her worries, make her feel safe. I wanted to be someone she could have faith in, the one who could make everything all right. But how could I when I didn't feel safely held, when I didn't have that much faith of my own? I too felt overlooked by God, more than ever now that Margaret had come into my life.

So, it was just me and my thoughts that evening and, when I couldn't stand it any longer, I decided to call Teresa.

"I hope I'm not disturbing you."

"Not at all," she said.

"I just wanted to find out how Margaret was doing, and to see if you noticed any change."

"No, everything is the same."

"How did dinner go?"

"Well, we gave her some mashed potatoes but she wouldn't eat them. She had a sip of apple juice is all. That's about it. The only difference was we didn't push her to eat tonight, as you suggested."

"How's she doing otherwise?"

"She seems a bit more relaxed than usual. Right now she's sitting on the floor making paper snowflakes."

Realizing this phone call was only accentuating the lack of progress, I said, "I know I told you not to expect anything, but I guess I got a little wishful. You did great by not pressuring Margaret to eat. Keep it up and get as much liquid into her as you can."

"I will."

"And of course, if you need me between now and Margaret's next appointment, don't hesitate to call."

She said, "Fine," clearly feeling a little let down but in no way directing her disappointment at me—for which I was deeply grateful.

"Can I talk to Margaret for a minute?"

"Sure."

I heard Teresa tell her it was me. It sounded as though Margaret had very little reaction to this news.

"Hello," she said in her tiny voice.

"Hi. How are you doing?"

"Fine."

"What are you up to?"

"Not much. Making Christmas decorations."

"Are you going to hang them on the tree?"

"No, just for fun."

"Do you remember what we talked about in my office?"

"Yes."

"So have you tried talking to Uncle Julio?"

She got very quiet and, after a pause, said, "Yes."

"Did you ask him to help you eat?"

"Yes."

"What did he say?"

Again she got very quiet, very still. I could feel her pulling in and reinforcing the etheric security blanket around her tummy.

"Margaret, I'd really like to know. What did he say?"

After more hesitation, she finally said, "Oh, this is silly."

"I don't think it's silly at all."

"Yes, it is," she replied, more energized, ready to move on.

"Okay, I have another question for you then. Do you believe in angels?"

"Yes."

"Have you ever seen any?"

"No."

"Well, I hear they're beautiful."

"Have *you* ever seen any?"

"Why, I'm looking at one right now, sitting on top of my Christmas tree."

"Not that kind," she squealed. "I mean the real kind."

"And what kind is that?"

"The real kind, like the angels around baby Jesus. Everybody knows about Jesus."

"Oh, they do, do they? And what exactly is it that they know about him?" I asked.

"That he helps everyone who asks him to," she replied.

"So, have you asked him for help lately?"

"No."

"Well then, why don't you try that? Why don't you ask him to help you eat? Just add it to your prayers. In fact, why not ask all the angels and all people who love you for help, okay?"

"Okay," she said, "that's easy."

She was clearly secure in her faith. What she took for granted and experienced without question was, for me, uncertain territory and a source of inner turmoil. I was completely taken in by her confidence.

We said good-bye and I listened for the "click" of her phone before hanging up. It was disturbing that she wouldn't tell me what Uncle Julio said when she asked him for help—if she even asked at all. Saying "this is silly" was her way of avoiding the issue. In no uncertain terms, she had just shut me out and was, in effect, telling me, *I won't let you in.* And I knew she never would . . . until I could believe too.

5

You do not have to be good.
You do not have to walk on your knees
for a hundred miles through the desert, repenting.
You only have to let the soft animal of your body
    love what it loves.
Tell me about despair, yours, and I will tell you mine.
Meanwhile the world goes on. . . .

—an excerpt from "Wild Geese" by Mary Oliver, *Dream Work*

Emptiness does not nourish the body or soul, it erodes the will to live. But for me, emptiness was a familiar sensation from the start. As a child I often threw my lunch away as I walked to school; it was too much trouble to carry and I never ate it anyway. I hated feeling full. Years later, I would wonder if this predilection was the trigger for an unrelenting case of edema that, at its apex, was so severe I couldn't fit into any of my clothing, shoes, or rings. The swelling happened overnight; I went to bed a size four and woke up a size ten. In the months following the onset of this condition, medical science failed me. All the specialists, all the tests, all the procedures, all in vain—the swelling did not subside. There was no rational explanation. . . .

Several months earlier, an aerobics instructor at the fitness center where I worked out suggested I see a spiritual healer and, willing to try anything, I took her advice. The morning of my appointment I caught an early train into the city, allowing myself time to walk from Grand Central Station to the upper West Side. I was insecure about the visit, not really sure what a faith healer was, or what they did, or what they knew, or what they could see. By the time I reached the West Side, I was convinced that if this healer was any good at all, she would surely discover what a horrible mess I was.

My concerns along these lines actually began the evening before; I made a point of eating a healthy dinner and deliberately avoided having dessert afterward. I certainly wasn't going to make it easy for her find out how bad I was. (I assumed she could use her X-ray vision to examine the contents of my digestive tract. "Aha! Chocolate!" she would say.)

Anxious to be healed, although I actually had no idea what that meant, I doggedly made my way uptown, vowing to do whatever she suggested. Arriving at the address nearly an hour ahead of time, I walked around the block several times— not wishing to appear overanxious, hoping to be the perfect patient. The appointment was for 8:30, so at precisely 8:15 I entered the building, quickly found her door, and took a deep breath before knocking. I waited and then knocked again. No one answered.

Deflated, I went back to the lobby and chose a discreet chair in the corner with a view of the entrance. Ten minutes later, a blond woman, obviously in a hurry, breezed through the front door and flew down the hall. She was not wearing business or medical clothing, but the two feathers in her hair seemed curiously juxtaposed to her relatively conservative outfit, and I knew she was the one I had come to see before I heard her unlock the door and enter the office. Although I didn't want to be late for the appointment, I decided not to go in right away, to give her time to settle in. I counted to one hundred three times before I approached her office and rang the bell.

"Come on in," I heard through the door. I entered and, from the back room, she said she'd be right with me.

"Okay," I responded, trying to sound relaxed and cheerful.

A few minutes later, the secretary arrived and greeted me pleasantly. Her name was Gwynn and, after getting settled at her desk, she gave me several forms to fill out: name, address, phone number, occupation, height, weight, reason for visit; pretty much a standard intake form. In filling it out, I felt compelled to confide certain intimate information about my condition, realizing that it was self-defeating to be anything less than forthright about who I was. My newfound candor was fueled by both a desire to get well and remain solvent; the session was not inexpensive. Although I would have paid any amount to get my health back, it seemed foolish to waste money or time being disingenuous about the nature of my condition.

Eventually the healer came into the waiting area, warmly introduced herself as Barbara, and, after shaking my hand, beckoned me to follow her down the hall to her "healing room." It was a simple room with two windows, a desk facing one of them, a white couch, and a professional massage table in the corner. I took a seat on the couch as Barbara sat down behind her desk and began looking over the completed intake forms, the expression on her face unreadable. On a nearby table I noticed ·a glass bowl filled with crystals of different shapes and colors. With this exception, there were no other New Age trappings in sight.

The office and Barbara's manner were both surprisingly professional, although it did little to relieve my trepidation. At the forefront of my fears was the notion I was about to be interrogated and my innermost secrets revealed. After asking some basic questions about my symptoms and health, Barbara had me stand up so she could read my chakras. Here it was, just as I feared, the X-ray vision. Of course, I knew what a chakra was— I had done a certain amount of reading on the subject—but I was enough of a neophyte to feel naked. She put as much distance between us as the room allowed and took several short, quick breaths, before looking me over. Curiously enough, I never for a moment doubted the validity of her work. I simply wondered what she was seeing, what was revealed.

She said that chakras were ethereal energy centers, spinning wheels of light, and that there were seven of them. She pointed to their locations with the calm, reassuring, seen-it-before manner of a scientist or doctor.

"The chakras on your back are all pulled in and kind of squished," she calmly reported. "These are your will centers. Are you scared?"

Fearing I was bad because my chakras were all screwed up, I said, "Yes, I've never done this before."

"Well, that's the way it looks."

That's it, I thought, I just failed the test. I got an "F" in personal energy. Secretly, I had been hoping she'd recognize something special in me, something unique. I was longing for someone to come into my life and tell me something good about myself, someone to tell me I was all right. Until that moment, I hadn't realized just how badly I needed external validation. A quiet storm washed away my denials and flooded me with sadness.

"I'd like you to get on the table now," she said.

I got on the table and laid down on my back, terrified of what she might discover next. Barbara started at my feet and began working her way up my body, performing what she called a chelation, touching all my joints and chakras. She didn't speak, and I mostly kept my eyes closed—which she said was optional. Overcome by curiosity, I peeked several times and saw Barbara moving her hands in a peculiar circular manner above my body, her eyes closed and fluttering, her breath rapid and stunted.

It occurred to me that I shouldn't be so concerned with what Barbara was doing and instead try to focus on what was happening with me. I made a strong effort to identify any subtle changes in the way I was feeling and was profoundly disappointed to discover I couldn't discern anything out of the ordinary: no new currents running through my body, no mystic forces, no voices, no angels, nothing.

When she was finished, Barbara asked me to remain on the table for a few minutes while she checked something in another room. After she left, I slowly opened my eyes and was surprised to find the plain white office was now filled with a beautiful green mist. The walls, the windows, everything in the room appeared green, almost as though there was a piece of tinted glass in front of my eyes. It didn't scare me or bother me in anyway, but I kept blinking in an attempt to make this inexplicable effect go away, trying to get my normal vision back.

When Barbara returned, I said, "There's something wrong with my eyes. The whole room looks green."

She smiled and calmly told me that I was in an altered state and seeing through my own energy field. "Have you ever seen this before?" she asked.

"Once," I said, "at a psychic fair."

Years earlier, before the edema, in a great deal of distress over the breakup of a long-standing relationship, I made a decision that was both in character and yet, I knew, totally outlandish. I honestly don't recall how I found out about it, if I read about it or whether somebody told me about it, but I decided to attend a New Age symposium that was being held on an upcoming weekend: crystals, auras, tarot cards, angels, Atlantis, etc. I was pragmatic enough not to tell anybody about my plans to attend but desperate enough to think I might find some sort of help there. At the time, my view of the New Age was what I imagined most people's view was: I thought there was probably something real there but suspected most of it was in the minds of the needy souls and true believers.

The symposium was held at a local Westchester hotel and was nothing like the fairs that are currently popular. It was more like a conference with a host of different speakers, each addressing small groups of 30 to 150 people. Most of the events took place in the main ballroom, but there were also smaller private rooms where you could go and have a personal reading, your tarot cards done, your palm read, or your astrological chart drawn up. But the major lectures and presentations were in the main ballroom, and I knew it was there I would feel the most comfortable, the most invisible.

There was a schedule posted in the lobby; at 2 P.M. a discussion about Atlantis, at 3 P.M. a lecture on crystals, and so on. I looked over the list of events and, while I thought it was all a little hokey, one event did catch my eye, something about a group reading. I was there, if for no other reason, to find relief from my recent heartbreak, and a group reading, whatever that was, seemed like a reasonable way to test the waters. Perhaps someone with no personal knowledge of my life could provide insight into the tatters of my broken heart and broken will. Maybe some authority figure could tell me whether or not I'd ever feel happy again, whether I'd ever have a healthy relationship, whether I'd ever be okay. I was there for the same reason people attend revivals and tent meetings, the same reason, years later, Ruth and Teresa would bring their daughters to see me. I was there to be healed; I was there to be saved.

Inconspicuously entering the main ballroom, I tried to blend in with the crowd farthest from the stage. Concerned that intimate and mundane facts about my life might at any moment be exposed, I took a seat in the second to last row— an expert at being invisible yet simultaneously miserable because no one noticed me. Naturally I secretly hoped to be discovered without having to draw attention to myself.

It was early and the man who was to conduct the "reading" had not yet arrived. Instead, a woman, to whom I was paying little attention, was in front of the group finishing her lecture on the lost city of Atlantis. Not particularly interested in the subject, I remained lost in thought, pretending to peruse the pamphlet I held in my lap. For no apparent reason, I happened to look up and saw what appeared to be a golden-yellow light coming out of the top of the lecturer's head. It was shaped like an ice cream cone. I had no idea what I was seeing.

Oddly enough, at that moment she shifted topics and started discussing chakras and auras—subjects I knew little or nothing about, although I had always harbored intense curiosity in these areas. I watched and listened with increasing interest as she began fielding questions from the audience. I sat there a dignified amount of time, letting several others go first, before hesitantly raising my hand. She eventually acknowledged me, and I stood up.

"What do chakras look like and what color are they?" I asked.

"Why do you ask? Are you seeing something?"

"Well, it looks like you have a glowing yellow ice cream cone on the top of your head."

She went over to one of the mirrored walls and looked at herself. "Oh, yes," she said, turning around toward me. "What you're looking at is my crown chakra which is shaped like a funnel."

She casually added, "You're quite perceptive, you know. Are you a sensitive?"

You've got to be kidding, I heard someone say or think, hoping it hadn't been me.

I felt a shiver go down my spine. Was I one of the people I'd come to see? Could that possibly be true? Although I had never seen a chakra before, or even knew what one was, the pervading feeling of being in a somewhat altered state felt remarkably normal.

"No, I don't think so," I responded.

"Oh," she said, shaking her head, appearing almost confused. "Oh well," her expression said and she nodded at another raised hand.

After fielding several more questions, the "Atlantis woman" departed and the "group-reading man" walked up to the stage. I immediately noticed a green and fuzzy glow around him that extended about six to eight inches from his skin, and was particularly dense toward the top of his body. I knew that this matched the "Atlantis woman's" description of an aura, and while I still didn't really know what to make of this phenomenon, I liked how it felt all the same. I was entranced, riveted.

After introducing himself, the first words out of his mouth were, "I teach healing, and the color of healing and health is green. People often see a green aura around me."

I remained silent and outwardly calm, but there was no doubt in my mind; I was actually seeing auras. Curiously enough, realizing I could see in this way was not that big of a deal, to me. It did nothing to blunt the fact that I was still feeling very lonely and small, my internal dialogue so overpowering that little of what happened that afternoon penetrated.

I snapped out of my melancholy when the "group-reader" started moving around the room, doing spontaneous readings. He would get close to a person, give a rapid-fire synopsis of his energy, and then quickly move on. Occasionally, he would point at an individual and describe the different spirits and departed loved ones that were surrounding them. This was promising, I thought; surely, when he comes my way, he'll notice my inner turmoil and offer some advice. Maybe my ancestors had the answers and could communicate them to me through him.

As it turned out, to my horror, every time he got near me he'd pick up his pace and quickly walk past. This happened two or three times, until I was convinced that he was actually physically repelled by my presence in some way. It was as though we were polarized like identical poles at the ends of two different magnets; his body language was that drastic. I wondered if anybody else noticed what was happening; it didn't appear as though he was having this trouble with any of the other members of the audience. Finally, after I had pretty much given up on the whole thing, he approached.

"Every time I get near you, there are these forces," he said. "There's a great deal of psychic activity in your vicinity. Did you know that?"

I shook my head.

"Well, there is. There seems to be a lot of dead people around you."

How very comforting, I thought.

"There's a woman here whose name is Rose," he continued. "Do you know someone named Rose?"

I said, "Yes, my mother's name is Rose."

"No, it's not your mother. The woman I'm seeing is much too old to be your mother."

I told him she was the only Rose I knew.

"Nonetheless, she's here and she says her name is Rose. Go home and ask your mother if she knows who this is because, as a matter of fact, the message is for her. Rose says to tell your mother to keep fresh cut flowers in the house—like they used to when she was a little girl."

I told him I'd be sure to bring this up later when I saw my mom. But I wasn't there for her benefit and, frankly, I found this a little annoying. I didn't want to be a conduit for somebody else's messages; I was the one who needed guidance.

"Isn't there any message for me?"

He seemed to get a little irritated at my asking this and said, "Okay, okay. There's another spirit here with another message. His name starts with A but I can't quite get it. Ann . . . Angel? I'm not sure. He's got a cane. His message is . . . is . . . also for your mother."

This was getting frustrating.

"Wait," he said and looked as though he were listening to some unheard instructions. Then, after a moment, he continued in a serious tone. "He wants you to tell your mother, whether she believes it or not, he's still with her, watching over her. Just like when she was a little girl. That's it."

That's it? That's not much. I sat through several more hours of lectures and workshops, but the remainder of the seminar was largely uneventful. Glowing auras and chakras popping out of people's heads wasn't the life-changing experience I was looking for that day. I wanted help. I wanted answers. I left the seminar dissatisfied and miffed about being some sort of spiritual messenger service for my mom. So much for a day at the fair. Naturally, I went straight to my mother's house on the way home.

She knew exactly who Rose was: her grandmother, my great-grandmother; they had been quite close until my great-grandmother's death. As it turned out, the inquiry ignited my mother's memory of her childhood. She said that Rose would take her out into the fields surrounding their home and they would pick wildflowers together and gather them into bouquets—Grandma Rose firmly believing that having fresh flowers in the house was good for the soul.

As for "Angel," he turned out to be Angelo, my mother's grandfather. In his latter years, he was rarely seen without his cane. He was an exceptionally talented and kindhearted man. A musician by inclination and trade, he took it upon himself to teach neighborhood children how to play an assortment of instruments, ultimately forming an orchestra—uniforms and all. He loved children and they loved him in return. He was an extremely important figure in my mother's life, his support and affection constant throughout her youth.

Although it was overwhelmingly clear she loved them both dearly, I couldn't recall her ever having spoken of Grandma Rose; I had no idea who she was—or maybe I just didn't remember. But the bond was strong and had transcended the years. I could feel all that and there was so much more to be felt. As my mother listened to the "messages" I brought home from the fair, her eyes glistened, revealing a tenderness I had too often overlooked.

I was still trying to blink the "green mist" away when Barbara smiled and said that all the chakras had colors, green being the color of the heart chakra on the emotional level—which didn't make much sense to me at that time, but sounded reassuring.

I got off the table and we sat on the couch together and talked for the remainder of the session. Barbara suggested I find time to meditate and recommended a book by Jack Schwarz called *Voluntary Controls*. When the subject of my love life arose, I told her my story without hesitation. She listened with great compassion as I recounted my long-term involvement with a man who lived a double life—supposedly in love with me while still dating someone else—and who was now stalking me. It was the first time I'd confided in anyone outside the circle of people who knew me, and it came as a great relief. Her response was totally unexpected. She softly said that this man and I were like two apples on a tree: I was ripe, luscious, and ready to be picked while he was still green and not, at this time, ready for the harvest. It was impressive that she found a way of describing the situation that didn't hurt or put anyone down. For some reason, that meant a great deal to me.

"And you should be grateful," she continued, "to the other woman he has feelings for. You should say a prayer and thank her. She has done you a great service."

It shocked me to hear her say this and, at the same time, at the core of my being, I understood exactly what she meant. I didn't have the strength or courage to free myself from the relationship and needed someone to solidify what I was unable to face. This man was not true to me or the other woman—never would be—and now she had accepted the weight of that burden.

With this still reverberating in my mind, Barbara said the reason she left the room was to consult an anatomy book. She'd seen an unfamiliar configuration in my pancreas and needed to refer to a medical diagram to find out what it was, to make sure it belonged there. It did. Physiologically, she felt the problem involved pancreatic function and suggested I drink sage tea several times a day.

I told her I'd have no problem doing that. When the session was over, I asked if she knew how many more visits I'd need.

"I think you'll just need to come once or twice more."

Before I left, Barbara said she saw me writing a letter, one that would initiate closure to the relationship I'd told her about. She said that once I did this, there would be a clear, clean break and this man would be out of my life for good. What she didn't seem to understand was that there was no way I was going to write him, particularly in view of the fact he was involved with another woman. In addition to my vulnerability, it would be cruel and humiliating for her, should she ever read it. I didn't want to hurt her; that wasn't what this was about. But what was it about? Although I still ached inside, something had definitely shifted. I wanted my life back.

On the train home, I couldn't stop thinking about the letter. I didn't know if this was some sort of psychic phenomenon or the power of suggestion. Either way, apparently I was the perfect subject because later that night I sat down and composed the most complete, open, and honest letter I'd ever written. In it, I told this man I loved him and that I always would. I acknowledged his choice to be with another woman and asked that he acknowledge my choices as well.

As I reread the letter, I realized it was written in such a way as not to be harmful to any of us: not him, not her, not me. Should she find it or he share it with her, she would not feel betrayed and at the same time, I was able to give him exactly what he seemed to need from me: my love.

I sent the letter and, almost immediately, the stalking came to an end: the notes on my car stopped appearing, there were no more visits, no more "coincidental" encounters, no more phone calls. I never saw or heard from him again.

I had two more appointments scheduled with Barbara and, in the interim, followed her instructions faithfully. The sage tea was unpleasant tasting but I drank it three times a day. At the end of the third appointment, Barbara informed me I wouldn't have to return and, while this was welcome news, a sense of incompleteness accompanied the sense of relief. The feeling went beyond the obvious concern that, as far as I could tell, nothing about my condition had changed;

the swelling, although not quite so severe, was still with me from head to toe.

After the final session, and unlike my previous visits, Barbara lingered in the office as I collected myself and prepared to sit up. A small dialogue had developed between us as the appointments went along, but I was still in unknown terrain. I remained on the table and Barbara stood next to me, neither of us saying anything. Finally, I opened my eyes and saw that hers were open as well . . . and she was studying me.

"What?" I said.

She appeared uncharacteristically hesitant, as though she was uncertain whether to speak or not.

"What? What is it?"

What she said came as a complete surprise. Her words went directly into my body, as though I was hearing my name, recognizing myself for the very first time. Softly she said, "Do you know that you are a healer?"

I didn't have a conscious response; I didn't say, "yes, I've always felt that way." I simply remained where I was, unable to respond or move—even after Barbara left the room. Warm, slow, silent tears slid down my face.

Some minutes later, Barbara returned with a brochure in hand and a long-winded apology, fearing that what she was about to suggest was a breach of the healer-patient relationship. She said, in spite of the fact that I was a client, she thought I should come to a workshop on healing she was teaching. It was obvious she was torn as to how to proceed, not wanting to appear self-serving but needing to genuinely communicate her sense that this was supposed to happen. "I know I shouldn't be doing this, but I really, really think you're supposed to come." I assured her that, as far as I was concerned, inviting me to her class was in no way unethical and, in fact, felt good, like being recognized.

I brought the brochure home and was unable to stop thinking about it. Actually, there was never any question about whether I was going to attend; I was just pretending to think about it. It would be many months before the edema would begin to subside, but gradually the condition improved. I took the workshop, which turned out to be my introduction to many years of studying, training, practicing, and eventually teaching healing. But the next step was to come before I was ready, a step I took with a tiny baby named Matthew Henry.

6

Belief is not an intellectual matter.

—from *A Prayer for Owen Meany* by John Irving

Spring is supposed to follow winter, as summer should lead to fall; life is certainly not supposed to end before it begins— as every mother knows. Matthew's mother, Natalie, worked upstairs in the insurance department and her husband Brian reported directly to me in training and development. Physically small, Natalie appeared to be the shy, demurring type, until you discovered her energy and resilience: she was always first on line to offer ideas or services and forever willing to "go the extra mile." In all the years I'd known her, I'd never seen her lose her love of life.

Brian was a family man and not a climber driven by ambition. He preferred skiing or woodworking in his garage to being stuck in an office. He had a good job, good salary, and good benefits, but the nine-to-five, jacket-and-tie treadmill was not really his cup of tea. Despite his thinning hair, he was a child at heart with blue eyes that held the mischievous twinkle of a six-year-old discovering his first frog, then hiding it in his sister's bed. I loved working with him. Reliably unpredictable, he infuriated me with his talent for making light of just about everything. I was forever harping on him to "be more serious and more professional," although his carefree nature was usually a breath of fresh air. I secretly wished I could be more like him.

He had taken time off to be with Natalie as she was about to give birth to their second child. He called the office to say that there had been trouble with the birth of their baby boy, whom they'd already named Matthew, and that the infant was in extremely serious condition. The prognosis quickly went from bad to worse when the baby began displaying symptoms of respiratory distress. Brian relayed the facts as casually as he could, but the situation had disrupted his usual easygoing manner and he was fighting to hold himself together.

"Is there anything I can do?" I asked.

"Like what?"

"I don't know. Anything."

He said that they were moving the baby to another hospital with a better neonatal-care unit that had more specialized equipment.

I sat alone in the office, unable to proceed with business as usual. Finally I cleared my desk, made a few phone calls, informed my staff of the situation, and in less than five minutes was on the road, on my way to Connecticut and the hospital where a baby was deciding whether to live or die.

The ride from White Plains to the hospital had taken a significant amount of time and, upon arriving, I was surprised to find Brian wasn't there yet. I assumed the paperwork for Natalie's transfer was holding them up.

The pediatric intensive care unit was relatively new and impressively constructed with thick glass walls so that you could see all the infants in their individual incubators. I spotted a nurse inside the unit and tapped on the glass to get her attention. Several minutes later, she emerged.

"Can I go in and see the Henry baby?" I wanted to get as close to him as possible. Maybe even touch him, hold him.

"Are you his doctor?"

"No."

"Sorry, no one's allowed in except the parents, and even they have to be under supervision."

She said the best she could do was go back in and point him out to me. I thanked her and she reentered the restricted area, rotated one of the incubators, and then rolled it directly in front of me on the other side of the glass partition. This was as close as I was going to get.

Matthew Henry was ever so tiny, with skin that looked almost translucent. His lips were thin and blue, and it was obvious he was suffering, each breath a labor, his little chest rising and falling, not on its own but with the help of machines. I couldn't tell if he was fighting for his life or surrendering to the pulse and rhythm of the equipment that held him in limbo. He was full of tubes.

The doctor said the baby had inhaled meconium while in the birth canal and that this was causing the respiratory distress. I thought it strange that my attention was drawn to his head and not his lungs, but I let it go, thoroughly overwhelmed by the situation and surroundings. It was all so still, so sterile, no flowers or cheery pictures. Pressing my hands against the wall of glass, I willed them to pass through the cold hard surface and touch the tiniest life I'd ever seen.

I don't know how long I stood there, but I was thoroughly lost in thought when Brian arrived, naturally surprised to see me. I told him I just had to come, and he said he understood, looking every bit a father who'd been told his son was not expected to live. I found myself thinking about running with Brian, which we often did after work. I remembered how we would increase our speed whenever we hit a hill, anxious to put difficulty behind us.

I only saw Matthew that one time while he was in the hospital. He suffered and struggled for weeks before Brian and Natalie, exhausted, relieved, and ultimately ecstatic, finally brought their new baby home. Knowing it would be many months before she'd be able to return to work, Natalie made a special trip to the office so we could all see Matthew. Everyone gathered around this miracle of life, oohing and ahhing, trying to get him to smile. His skin was still inadequate to hide his little blue veins.

I patiently waited for my chance to hold him, only to discover that, when I finally had Matthew in my arms, I was not overcome with the rapture of new life. In fact, I had to hide my concern and discomfort. I was having the same gut reaction I'd had in the hospital months before; there were no ethereal voices, no mystical visions, no angels, no guides—just a nagging ache in my belly: *there's something wrong with his head.*

While the last thing I wanted to do was set off any unnecessary alarms, at the appropriate moment, as carefully as I could, I suggested to Brian that they get a second opinion about their baby. It came as an immense relief when he and Natalie accepted the suggestion and took Matthew to their pediatrician to be re-evaluated. Once again, however, the doctor assured them their baby was fine. Instead of easing my anxiety, I grew even more concerned and urged them to seek yet another opinion. I couldn't have been more uncomfortable, with my unsubstantiated doomsday prognostications, but Brian and Natalie were the tenacious type and, having doubts of their own, had already decided to take Matthew to a top neurosurgeon in New York City. The examination, and ensuing tests, confirmed the existence of an aneurysm in his brain—impossible to reach surgically and, if ruptured, deadly.

That is where my direct involvement ended. Matthew was never really my patient; I knew him only as a friend's newborn baby, and contact with his parents dwindled after I left the company and our lives moved on. Matthew would share his life with the specter of death that had taken residence in the center of his brain. And I would carry that knowledge with me through all the years, prayers, and children that would follow him into my practice.

Although it was difficult, because it was unsubstantiated, speaking up about Matthew's condition was not optional; I could easily recall a moment in which I had failed to speak up, or at least not loudly enough.

Having worked many years as a psychotherapist at Pace University, I was full of expectation when I accepted a position in the human resource department of a large, well-known telecommunications company. It was my first excursion outside of academia, and I was unprepared for the reality that, in the business world, the focus is confined to the basics: money, money, money, make the sale, make the sale, make the sale. As this company was a relatively new player, it was particularly aggressive in its approach, hellbent on making its way to the top. My position in training and development required a good deal of interaction with the employees, and, while counseling wasn't part of my job description, people soon began confiding in me—for which I took a little heat from above. Actually, I was under the impression that my boss would likely use these unauthorized, albeit informal, sessions against me, but I couldn't stop the flow of people in and out of my office.

One of the more frequent visitors was an executive vice president in charge of marketing. With much on his mind and shoulders, he had begun seeking refuge in my office, claiming he was being scapegoated as the one responsible for the company's losses that year. In addition, he had recently become a father but was experiencing this as an added pressure rather than as a blessing. As the weeks and months went by, he continued to confide in me, and it became obvious to me that he was slipping into a severe depression. It was clear that he felt trapped with no way out and no way to save face. I urged him to get help, but he said the only help he needed was a sales quota sheet that matched the company's projections. It ultimately reached the point where I was convinced he was going to attempt suicide—I was sure of it—and decided to tell my boss. Her response, rather snippily delivered, was that I should mind my own business.

Certain this was a life-and-death situation, I defied the sacred code of the corporate culture and went over her head.

"This man believes the department's financial failure is all his fault," I said to my boss's superior. "If we don't lift some of the blame, there's a good possibility he'll attempt suicide. This man's at the end of his rope."

Once again, I was told I was out of line and my superior's superior refused to hear another word about it.

"For goodness sake, he just had a new baby. This is his life we're talking about, a family's life! Someone should call his wife and offer some kind of support or advice."

"Based on what? Just leave it alone."

I couldn't and, hoping I'd find an elevated sense of compassion at the top, I went to the head of the company. "Tom's in real trouble. Somebody has got to do something."

The CEO listened with greater patience than his staff and then calmly informed me I had an attitude problem. He said I was way, way out of line and that management had been complaining about me—letting me know, in no uncertain terms, that my job was in jeopardy.

"Tom is no concern of yours and his job performance is none of your business. Besides, they just had a new baby," he scolded me. "There's no way I'm going to call his wife with your 'impressions.' "

Having been put in my place and then firmly dismissed, I quickly left the office and then the building. At least it was Friday and I could escape the hell I was working in. I would soon regret my acquiescence. When I returned to work on Monday, everyone was talking about Tom. He had entered his garage that weekend—I didn't catch which day—closed the door behind him, started the car, and never came out. *A brand-new baby.*

I headed directly to the top man's office and told him that I thought he and the company had unfairly made a scapegoat of a man with enough conscience to believe it. I said it was hard to imagine this organization's money problems were all one man's fault and, even if that was the case, life can't be measured in terms of dollars and cents and, finally, that I didn't know how to work in a place where a human life had no value.

He again said that I was a troubled employee, that I was the problem.

"I'm the problem?! I'll tell you what the problem is, it's questionable business practices, that's what the problem is! You're asking me to train people to sell your product even if it kills them! You just want to grab dollars quickly and at any cost. And now a man is dead. If you don't do something and change the way you do business, I don't know what I'm going to do."

He said I wasn't going to do anything; I was a disturbed individual with no support left in the organization. Reeling from this, I looked him square in the eye and shot from the hip. "You know what I think, I think *The New York Times* would be interested in the way you do business around here."

His cold and instant response was, "You're fired."

"Fired!? I quit! I don't want to spend another second in this place."

I wish I had turned like a soldier and boldly marched out of his nicely appointed office, but I was shaking like a leaf and it took all my strength just to get through the door and down the hall. As quickly as I could, I cleared my desk, gathered my things, proceeded to the elevator, got into my car, and then started to cry so hard I could barely drive. For the first time in my life, I had nowhere to go, no job, no insurance, and no security. And all that would have been just fine, if only I'd stood all the way up when it mattered. *A new baby.*

7

A discouraging phone call from Teresa reminded me of my fussy eating habits, which frustrated my mother when I was Margaret's age. In the ensuing battle of wills, I would choose hunger over swallowing something I didn't like and end up getting my unfinished dinner served to me the next morning. Uncle Don was the only one who could get me to eat when I didn't want to; I would eat whatever he placed in front of me, which, of course, only added to my mom's frustration. But Uncle Don and I had a secret, something I believed she knew nothing about. He called it the "Clean Your Plate Club." Whenever he baby-sat, at mealtime he would draw a face or cartoon character on my plate before putting the food on it. In order to see the whole picture, I had to eat everything on the dish.

According to Teresa, Margaret was doing anything but cleaning her plate. I reminded myself that I had awoke that morning determined to take a break from the mysteries of the universe and tried to get more in the moment and concentrate on the 10K race I had entered. But I could still see Margaret's big blue eyes in my mind, only now they appeared larger than they were in real life, eyes that had seen more than they were revealing.

So the Clean Your Plate Club, and not the race, was what I was thinking about as I joined the other runners, also early arrivals, on the registration line. It was a crisp morning with wispy clouds and crackly air, surprisingly warm, the kind of day that doesn't belong to the season. I put the top down on my car before leaving for the race; it was that kind of day.

I don't remember exactly when I started running or why. Although I was a decent athlete in college and liked sports, I wasn't interested enough to pursue running as anything more than a way to burn calories or let off steam. Now I mostly run because I can. I don't have to adjust my schedule, or make an appointment, or find a partner, or buy special equipment, or anything; I don't even need good weather. It's one area of my life in which I feel very much in control. And I like the solitude.

Although I don't necessarily feel great after every run, I am often left with a clearer sense of what's going on inside myself, not surprised when buried feelings of fear, anger, or even sadness, come to the surface. The opposite also happens. Sometimes, although not often, I'll complete a run and be unable to recall at all what I have been thinking about. But by far my favorite runs are the ones in which time dissolves, and I am home before I know it.

This day, time had not yet dissolved as I left the registration area and mingled in the crowd. I hadn't entered the race to compete or see how fast I could go, which, to some extent, isolated me from the other participants. I had come to think of competition as something to be avoided, my days of competitive racquetball not so distant that I could not recall when winning was all-important.

At one point during a championship match, my coach (and former boyfriend) instructed me to adopt what he called "a game face," warning me not to talk to my opponent or, under any circumstance, to smile. It was that mindset, and the failed relationship that intertwined, that quelled my interest in competitive events. But for some reason, when I noticed the ad for this 10K race in a local newspaper, I wanted to run in it despite my misgivings. In truth, I was hoping to meet someone: maybe a new friend, a fellow runner or, not that far in the back of my mind, a great guy.

Although it wasn't far from where I lived, I had never been to the town that was hosting the event and was unfamiliar with the course. I deliberately didn't tell anyone I was signing up for the race so there'd be no distractions if Mr.

Right happened to go jogging by. When the morning of the race came and my neighbor Lynn pulled into her driveway as I was backing out of mine, I wasn't prepared for the plan to fall apart so quickly.

"Where are you off to at this hour of the morning?" she asked.

"The Jan Peak Race up in Peekskill."

"That's great, I want to go too! Can you wait while I change into my running clothes? I'll be quick about it, won't take a minute."

"I'd prefer not to wait. I want to get there early."

"No problem," she responded cheerfully. "I'll look for you when I get there."

The race began in front of the running supply store that was cosponsoring the event, the store where all the participants were supposed to pick up their commemorative T-shirts. Although I arrived and was on line early, by the time my turn came they had inexplicably run out of the shirts. After registering, there was little for me to do besides mill around, uncomfortable to be an outsider within this community of runners. Wearing high-tech, high-fashion gear, everyone seemed to know each other or be a part of some group or organization. I was wearing old cotton running shorts and a cotton T-shirt.

The conversations that swirled around were mostly about past competitions and fastest times. I tried to be engaging, but the other runners were largely focused on their individual and group strategies. With little hope of interaction before the race, I sat on the curb and started to retie my shoes for the third time. *Keep your pace*, a distant yet familiar voice whispered. What is that supposed to mean? *Find your place*, was the non-response. As I sat there, the not-particularly-poetic "keep your pace, find your place" began to repeat itself in my mind. I looked up and saw Lynn standing there.

"Hi, I made it!" she said, smiling and confident.

In addition to her high-tech running outfit, she was holding one of the T-shirts they'd supposedly run out of. "How did you get a T-shirt?" I asked, trying to keep the disappointment and annoyance from my voice.

"Well, I pretty much know everybody here, I guess," was Lynn's answer, and it made perfect sense; she being the considerably more avid runner than I—not to mention the faster—knew people, and when you know people you get T-shirts.

Keep your pace.

I'm trying.

I looked at Lynn and said, "I feel bad. I know it's just a T-shirt but it's the story of my life: Follow the rules, be a good girl, show up on time, and still no T-shirt."

"Wait here a second," she said, not completely understanding the complexity of my disappointment. "I'll get you one."

She trotted off and in less than five minutes was back draping a T-shirt over my shoulder. As we headed to the parking area to put the shirts in our cars, I realized it was nice to have someone to talk to. I was glad Lynn was there and thanked her, although she mistook what for.

"It's just a T-shirt," she said. "We should start warming up."

Despite all the advice and admonitions about warming up, I've always had an aversion to stretching. Although I try to do it, mostly to prevent injuries, it doesn't loosen me up, and this day was no exception. I dutifully went through the motions along with Lynn, extending quads, calves, and hamstrings, but it did little to relieve the stiffness I felt in my joints and muscles.

As we lined up for the start, I turned to Lynn and said, "I know I can't keep up with you, and I don't want to even try. I'll meet you at the finish line."

Lynn seemed relieved to hear this, obviously not wanting to be held back from running her race either, and inched her way to the front of the pack, where the faster runners were still stretching and mentally preparing themselves. This was only the second year the town had hosted the race and the event had not attracted a very large field, maybe a hundred or so. At the sound of the gun, the front runners took off and seconds later we were all in motion.

As we ran through the downtown area, I started to get caught up in the sound of all the pounding feet and applauding spectators. Having only run in one other race, I had forgotten about the impact of a crowd. The little voice in my head kept reminding me not to try to impress anyone, which was good advice. I was more than a little tight and concerned I'd pull a muscle or burn out early if I tried to match the strides of the runners who had surged ahead of me.

As soon as we left the downtown area the course immediately went uphill and then turned a corner. Lynn disappeared around the turn, and I never regained sight of her. Because the course was so curvy, I wasn't always able to see the runners ahead of me. Seeing them is an easy way to stay on course. It occurred to me that I might not know which way to go without someone to follow.

Keep your pace, find your place.

I'm trying.

There were no longer crowds of spectators lining the road, although many of the people who lived along the race route had come out to watch from their lawns and decks, sitting on blankets and even rocking chairs. Some waved and I waved back. There were several water stations along the way and an occasional lemonade stand manned by tiny, hopeful faces. The course led us through mostly working-class neighborhoods, winding through the grounds of the high school and past several churches. It struck me, without causing much concern at first, that a steady stream of runners were buzzing past me. In time it became more difficult to ignore the passing parade, and the impetus to go faster and try to keep up grew stronger. "Keep your pace, find your place" echoed in my head.

I was running conservatively but strong, not straining or huffing and puffing, and moving at a reasonable clip—or so I believed until a ten-year-old boy blew past me on a straight-away. I should have guessed this was but a prelude to what was to come. Within minutes young and old were passing me on both sides and it was getting more difficult by the second to keep my cool, let alone my pace. So many runners had gone by, in fact, that I was relatively certain I was at the back of the pack when I heard someone else gaining on me. It was an older, gray-haired man who, although he appeared to be moving slowly, passed me with ease. The fact that he had to make more of an effort than the ten-year-old offered little consolation. I later found out that, at eighty-one, he was the oldest competitor in the race.

Running at my own pace, comfortable with my stride and breath, I settled into a nice, smooth rhythm, a little faster than my normal solitary pace. "Keep your pace" was starting to make sense when I heard an odd sound behind me. A bicycle? A skateboard? Roller blades? Whatever it was, it was moving at a pretty good clip and almost on me. I was anything but relieved when a woman pushing a baby jogger whizzed past me and out of sight.

The next people to pass were a father and son. "Move it!" I heard the boy's father say. "You can go faster."

Tears were streaming down the boy's face as he struggled to keep up.

"Come on, we're pulling up the back of the pack," the boy's father continued, pushing his son.

The boy gulped, "Dad, please. I can't. I really can't."

"Come on, truck it! You're going to embarrass us, for Christ's sake."

"Hey, let up," I whispered, not sure if I really intended the man to hear it. Despite the boy's distress, they were soon out of sight. It seemed even reluctant children could outrun me.

Keep your pace, find your place.

I'm doing the best I can.

About midway through the race, I noticed that it had been a while since anyone had passed me and although I could hear footsteps behind me, they never seemed to get any closer. Apparently, we were moving at about the same speed. A quarter mile later, just before the road made another sharp turn to the right, I caught a glimpse of several runners ahead of me just before losing sight of them again. When the road straightened out again, I was on their heels and, without increasing my speed, began to pass them. I assumed they must be slowing down, maybe because they started faster than they were used to. I kept moving and another half mile or so down the road, I came upon the "coach" and his son. They were standing off by the side of the road, the boy broken down in tears, saying over and over, "I can't do it. I just can't do it."

As I passed, I caught their eye and urged them on. "Come on guys, you can do it." Then softly to the boy's father, I said, "Let the boy set the pace," hoping he would hear me this time.

I started passing more and more people and figured that I was no longer at the back of the pack. Having not pre-run the unmarked course, I had no idea where in the race I was. When I came up next to a man who looked like a seasoned competitor, I said, "How's it going?"

"Good, and yourself?"

"Very good. How much farther?"

"The finish is just around the corner," he said. "Now's the time to turn on the juice if you have any left. Want to sprint to it?"

"No, I think I'll just keep my pace."

"Well, okay, see you at the finish."

He took off in a sprint and began to pull away but then just as quickly slowed down. When I caught up to him, I asked what had happened.

"Got a terrible stitch," he grimaced.

A stitch is a painful side-ache that takes your breath away, a common pitfall for runners. "I hate those," I said as I returned to the race, stepping it up a little as the finish line came into sight.

I heard Lynn's voice before I saw her on the sidewalk, cheering me on. After catching my breath, I joined her and the other spectators cheering for the remaining runners. Lynn introduced me to several of her friends, all of whom were very gracious. But I wanted to go home.

"I can introduce you to lots more people if you stay." Lynn was enjoying herself and clearly not ready to leave.

"Thanks," I said. "I'll see you back home."

On the drive home, I thought about the boy in the race whose desire to please his father had taken him to the verge of collapse. I thought that it was probably the desire to please, and not the physical excursion, that caused him to lose his will, and maybe that's how Margaret lost hers. If something as innocuous as adjusting my stride to run with a friend was too much of a concession for me, then Margaret's predilection to continually alter her behavior to accommodate whoever entered her sphere had to be too much for her. We both had to learn to leave pleasing behind and let experience unfold like a good run does.

I arrived home and didn't bother to change out of my running clothes, immediately heading for the phone to call a friend who was an experienced therapist. She is often out of town, her services being very much in demand, and it was a relief to hear her real voice instead of the usual answering machine message. I told her I had seen a little girl earlier in the week who was having trouble eating. This was the first I'd spoken of Margaret to anyone.

"The problem seems to be in her solar plexus and I'm pretty sure it's an invasion or boundary issue," I confided.

"Have you talked to her parents about this?"

"According to the child's mother, neither she nor her husband have any knowledge of an abusive incident. Either they don't know about it, they're in denial, or it didn't happen. One of their doctors explored this area as well, but nothing seemed to come of it."

"What do you think?" she asked.

"I think there's a distinct possibility there was some form of abuse, be it physical, emotional, or sexual. I don't know the specifics, but I mentioned to the mother that I felt the girl's relationship with her uncle was not normal." As the words came out of my mouth, an odd thing occurred. I realized I knew more about Margaret's situation than I had previously thought and I was able to spontaneously describe particulars, many of which I found disturbing. Dumbfounded by the depth of my own knowledge and disturbed by its nature, I told her everything about the case, including my impressions.

"It sounds like there's a severe problem," she responded, "and you have some very serious work to do."

"Yes, that's how it seems to me, too. But I'm at a complete loss as to how to proceed."

"Well, don't worry about it, Rosie," she said. "I know you'll do fine."

This was not what I had in mind. I was hoping she'd tell me exactly what to do and how to do it—and then guarantee it would work.

I thanked her for having faith in me and the conversation ended there, "you'll do fine," reverberating in my head, sounding very much like "keep your pace, find your place." Only now there was no one to follow. I was very much in the lead, on an unmarked course, with no idea what was ahead. But somehow I had stumbled into the subtle power of believing in myself and knew this would change everything.

8

Teresa and Margaret were right on time. Hearing the minivan pull into the parking lot, I was out of my chair and at the door in time to watch them exit the car. I was overcome with a desire to run to Margaret but, not wanting to appear overanxious, ran only halfway toward them and then slowed my steps as I approached.

Teresa said, "You remember Roseanne, don't you, Margaret?"

It was one of those polite things one sometimes says, but I was taken aback by it, feeling that the question failed to acknowledge the intimacy I assumed already existed between us. Or was I being too sensitive? It was reassuring when Margaret threw her arms around me and gave me a big hug.

Once inside, I asked Margaret if she managed to eat at all that past week and she made shy, sheepish sounds, not saying yes or no. I asked Teresa if there had been any change, and she said there had not been. No miracle. No magic.

It was nine days before Christmas. Margaret was looking all the more gaunt and weary from another week without food, and Teresa was even more frightened. She fervently did not want to see her daughter enter the hospital which, for Teresa, had become the symbol of the end of hope.

Once again, for her own reasons, Teresa did not have the need or desire to be in the office during the session and chose to sit in the waiting room.

"You're more than welcome to join us if you change your mind," I said.

"Thanks. Come get me if you need me."

"Margaret, are you okay being alone with me?" I asked in a funny little voice.

"Yes."

"I'm probably going to do more silly, strange things."

She giggled, took my hand, and accompanied me into the office. Teresa wished me luck with a hopeful nod as I closed the waiting room door.

"Do you have any questions about anything that happened the last time you were here?"

At first Margaret shook her head "no" and then, as though she had something of a revelation, said, "Yeah, I want to know why you moved your hand over me like this." She waved her hand through the air in a circular motion.

"I was helping to charge up one of your chakras which, you might remember, is an energy center. I cleared it up so you'd have more energy. You've been tired a lot, haven't you, sweetie?"

"Yes."

"Well, that's what I was trying to help you with."

The look on her face told me this was all the explanation she required.

"I'd like you to get right up onto the table today. Is that okay?"

She said yes and, with a little help, climbed up onto the old oak table. She knew what to do from the last visit and immediately laid down on her back with her arms at her sides, legs straight. I was struck by how exceptionally tiny she appeared on the adult-size table, how extremely fragile.

I performed the same procedures as in the first session, working with her energy and talking to her about what I was doing. We went through the chakras, my hand no closer than six inches from her body, and for the most part she played along to please me. After awhile I had her close her eyes.

"Do you feel that?"

"No."

"Do you feel this?"

"No."

Occasionally I'd tickle her foot. "Do you feel that?"

"Yes," she said through a thousand tiny giggles.

"See, you do feel something," I told her, and she laughed some more. "Can you feel this?"

Lightly placing my hands on her feet, this being the standard place to begin a chelation, I carefully cupped my fingers around her toes, my thumbs on the solar plexus reflex points on her soles, and held her in this manner for about five minutes. I let the energy flow, curious as to what her reaction might be, since she showed no sign of discomfort. When I was satisfied, I moved to her ankles and remained there a moment. Then I placed my hands on her knees and then her hips, working on one side then the other. With each move, I told her where I was going to touch her and asked her permission before proceeding, so as not to disturb her energy or psyche. I remained at her hips for several minutes, fully expecting her to react to my proximity to her midsection. When I felt she was comfortable with this, I asked, "What are you feeling?"

"Nothing," she said.

"Are you okay?"

"Yes, I'm fine."

She appeared to have no external reaction to my touch so, still avoiding direct contact with the solar plexus region, I placed my hand a couple of inches above her belly button, just below her third chakra. Her energy immediately pulled away, just as it had in the first session when I tried to touch her from across the room.

"You feel that, huh?"

"No, I'm fine."

Even with her eyes closed, she would wince every time my hand came too close. Eventually she started saying she felt something when I touched certain other chakras, although I couldn't tell whether she was actually allowing herself to be more sensitive or just playing along. I took it as a sign she was feeling more comfortable and hoped she might soon tolerate my touching her midsection—not just energetically but physically. When I thought she was ready, I said, "I would like to touch your tummy chakra, Margaret. Can I do that?"

Her eyes still closed, she nodded, and I moved my hand into the sensitive area. She didn't flinch, so I slowly brought it a little closer.

"Are you okay, honey?"

"Yes."

"Good. I've got an idea. Let's try something a little different."

I handed her Bear, then helped her sit up on the table and began working from behind. "I'm here with you. I won't do anything to you without your permission. I will stay here with you until you are ready. You decide what happens to you." I said it once out loud and then over and over again in my mind. With my arms fully around her and her arms fully around Bear, we proceeded an inch at a time.

"Are you still okay?"

She nodded, a little nervous, not in any physical pain, but every cell in her body reacting. She let go of Bear and he lay limp on her knees.

"All right, then, I'm going to bring my hand a little closer."

We went on like this until I was just an inch or so above her midsection, the closest I'd been. We stayed this way for two or three minutes, until I felt her system grow calm, then I began to traverse the final inch and actually touched her stomach, ever so lightly, with both hands. She didn't appear tense or upset, she wasn't even wincing, but she was definitely not a child at ease. *I'm here with you. I won't touch you without your permission.*

I continued to move up her body, touching not only her third chakra but also her heart chakra, her throat chakra, and then the temples on the side of her head, noticing the specific way each chakra responded.[1] When I was satisfied she was as relaxed, balanced, and energetically charged as possible, I returned to the third chakra and maintained physical contact.

Anticipating her arrival that day, I helped myself to a couple of candy canes from the realtor's Christmas tree upstairs. It was just a hunch, but I reached over and picked them up off the desk. As casually as I could, I unwrapped one and started sucking on it. Margaret sat up to see what I was doing.

"Well, how rude of me. Here I am eating a candy cane and I didn't even think to offer you one."

I peeled the other candy cane's wrapper back and handed it to her, then sat behind her on the massage table. Her back to my chest, she was unaware of my attempt to clear her third chakra. She took the candy, which she did not seem at all interested in, and held it in her fist as though it was anything but food, virtually repulsed by it. I continued to lick my candy cane, oohing and ahhing about how good it was, but she wasn't fooled, so I focused all my attention on the trauma in her third chakra, my arms firmly around her, my touch no longer tentative. I worked in silence, lifting the dark, cloud-like energy out of her field. After about ten minutes, without realizing what she was doing, and to my amazement, she casually brought her candy cane to her mouth and, a moment later, actually began to suck on it. I watched in stunned silence as she swallowed and then swallowed again, apparently having no problem with it whatsoever!

I was ready to jump for joy when she suddenly shifted positions and I had to let her go so she could make the adjustment. The instant she moved away, she began to gag and again appeared visibly repulsed by the candy. I took her back in my arms and, oddly enough, she began to eat it once more as though nothing had happened. What was this all about?

Experimenting, I got up and moved away from the table, all the while sucking on my candy cane. I watched as she pulled the candy from her mouth, choking. "What's the matter? Don't you like it any more?"

"I don't know," she whined, obviously confused and somewhat disconcerted.

"Well, it's okay," I said.

When I returned and held her in my arms, she automatically began to suck on the candy again. I tried this several times, careful to make sure she didn't notice what I was doing—I needed her reactions to remain spontaneous. Sure enough, within my field she could suck on the candy, outside of it she could not—and I knew it was the energetic, not the physical, holding that was making the difference. If nothing else, this confirmed that what I was doing was having an effect, a positive effect, but not a lasting one.

But as wonderful as it was, the work with the candy cane was only a clue to what was going on with Margaret and by no means a cure. Although I was able to clear her third chakra, it was extremely tenuous. As soon as I walked away, the "darkness" would return. It was as though, somehow, I was protecting her—as if there were something negative that couldn't get to her when she was enveloped in my field.

I had her lie on the table again and touched her feet, as I had before. This time I was overwhelmed by what I experienced; call it a metaphor if you choose, but for me it was terribly real. It began as a feeling that registered in the back of my mind and gradually evolved into an extraordinarily solid vision. As much as I didn't want to see his fist in her third chakra, it was there nonetheless, holding on, unrelenting, and deliberate. He was standing at Margaret's side, clear as a bell, invading her ability to eat by literally squeezing her tiny tummy. Good old Uncle Julio.

I didn't see him with what one would call physical vision and was thankful not to, but what I "saw" was real enough, the "metaphor" of a man's hand helping me connect with the idea of invasion and abuse. As I surrendered to the experience, the image began to change and the fist became an energetic configuration of dark grayish strands, like the roots of a tree, entwined in her abdominal muscles. And like roots sucking water from the ground, these were sucking the life out of

Margaret. The more I focused on the dark energy, the sharper my view became and the more useful the information.

Whether this was symbolic of some previous invasion or an actual vision was not of particular importance. What was important was the knowledge that, one way or another, Uncle Julio was directly and purposely impeding Margaret's ability to survive. This was why she couldn't eat, or even attempt to eat.

My reaction was in no way professional. I was furious, utterly consumed by anger. I could think of nothing more despicable: a full-grown man squeezing the life out of a defenseless child. There was no corresponding picture of sexual or physical abuse, but the sight of Uncle Julio in the act of preventing Margaret from eating was all my outrage needed.

No one gets to intentionally supplant love and nurturance with desperation: especially not with a child. I was particularly incensed at his cowardice for retreating every time I put my energy between his and hers. I knew he was using her, but it took me a moment to understand what exactly it was he had in mind. Then I got it: *Oh my God, he wants her to be with him. He wants her to care for him just as she did when he was alive. He's lonely and longs for her company. He actually wants her to die.*

I didn't try to pull the dark roots out from the top as you would a weed but instead directed my efforts to the deepest part of her third chakra where the tips of the roots held fast. I touched each of them with "light." Whether it was the light of wisdom, the light of understanding, or the light of God was immaterial. All that mattered to me was that the roots were slowly beginning to recede. I gradually expanded the light until all the inappropriate energy was completely out of her third chakra, then out of her physical body, and ultimately out of her energy field, a full eight to ten feet away.

I should have felt some sort of compassion for Uncle Julio, for his loneliness and great need. Yet all I could feel was contempt and fury at this ghost of a man, and the certainty it was time to move to the next step. Margaret's problems were the result of a distorted relationship with her uncle, which explained why the work with her had been largely ineffective and transitory. What was needed was a relational healing, some sort of group therapy, and I knew I couldn't do it alone.

The image appeared almost immediately—just behind Margaret's head, a little to her left—a steadfast radiance, an intense, comforting sense of confidence and grace emanating from it. I was consumed by gratitude and an indescribable sense of relief—relief that released me from all mental gymnastics and analytical thinking, freed me from the pressure to get things right. As with Julio, the image could be viewed in more than one manner. In one perspective, it was an opalescent, brilliant blaze of light, soft and easy to look at. In another, it was the Christ.

Although vague and incredibly subtle, he appeared in the form I knew from my childhood: a bearded man with brown hair and soft features wearing a white robe, similar to the traditional version, the one of him after he had risen—a light being, not a man. At that moment, I realized I was also completely engrossed with Margaret; everything about her fascinated me: her tiny fingernails and light blond lashes, the dark circles under her eyes, the freckles on her nose, her shallow breathing. I noticed everything about her. I felt as deeply transported by the vision of Margaret as I was by the brilliant light that surrounded us. Every cell in my body began to tingle, alive with a force that opened not only my vision but my soul. I was so thoroughly enraptured by this experience that it came as something of a shock to realize this wasn't solely a spiritual event, it was also a human one. I was angry, angry at Uncle Julio, and began to silently rage at him: *Get out of here, Uncle Julio! Leave her alone! Whoever you are, get out!* The force of my being fully unleashed, I was not acting, role-playing, or hesitating in any way.

Get out! my mind shouted. *Get out!* And lo and behold,

Julio started moving away. *Get out, get out, get out!* And he moved farther away. *Get out and stay out!* I was screaming at the top of my lungs without making a sound, and Julio was in retreat, unable to withstand the unbridled power of pure intent. Fury became my ally, anger my partner, outrage my guide. The fire in my belly ran through my body and shot up my back, yet it was not the anger that was significant but the genuine expression of it that mattered.

Despite the intensity of the moment, Margaret remained motionless on the table, eyes closed, unaware of the silent battle raging just above her. A battle we were not necessarily winning. For despite my ranting and raving, Julio's retreats were only temporary. He would back off when confronted and return as soon as I moved from Margaret's side. I tried this several times and, as with the candy cane, if the distance between Margaret and I exceeded more than six feet, he would return.

Get out of here, Julio! Just get the hell out! I bellowed internally. But each time he would retreat, moving a short distance away, where he'd await my departure. Frustrated, I searched for an idea, for another approach. Obviously this tortured man needed love and compassion or else he wouldn't be doing this—not if he knew better, was loved better. So again I turned to the Holy Presence for help, and this time I asked on behalf of all of us: Margaret, Uncle Julio, and me.

Julio, move toward the love. It will help you. I silently repeated this again and again, but it was no use; he wasn't responding, and I couldn't figure out why. All the ingredients were present, the truth exposed in a radiance of overwhelming splendor, the moment at hand. Why wasn't this working? What was missing? I was out of ideas and beginning to despair when I remembered I wasn't alone in this. Help was here for me, too. I had my hands on her feet.

"Do you want to play a game?" I asked Margaret.

She opened her eyes and said yes. I could tell by the sound

of her voice that, despite my efforts to hide it, she was aware of the rise in my energy level.

"Well, it's different from the games we played before. Is that okay?"

"How do you play?"

"It's easy. All you have to do is repeat whatever I say. Think you can do that?"

"Yes."

"Good. Oh, but there is one small rule."

"What is it?"

"Whatever I say, you have to say it louder than I do. That should be fun, don't you think?"

She agreed, but I knew this wasn't going to be easy for her. Up until this point, I hadn't seen her do anything loud or obnoxious, let alone unruly. Yet that's exactly what I needed from her. It was essential she leave behind the perfectly behaved, exceptionally quiet child she believed she should be.

"Do you remember how we asked Uncle Julio to help you eat, but it didn't work?"

"Yes."

"Well, I think I figured out how to make it work this time. You want to eat a great big Christmas dinner, don't you?"

"Yes."

"And you love Uncle Julio, right?"

"Yes."

"Well, Uncle Julio loves you too and the love between the two of you will always be there." I said this knowing I was reinforcing the connection between them, but hoping it would be understood that from now on, it had to be a healthy connection. The love could remain but that didn't mean Margaret had to tolerate emotional abuse and invasion. In the following minutes, I tried my very best, on a six-year-old level, to deliver this message.

"Does that make any sense to you?"

"I think so."

"Okay, then let's play. Just repeat everything I say and feel free to add anything you want to say, too. Here we go. 'Uncle Julio, let me go so I can eat.'"

Margaret remained silent; it was obvious she was going to have a great deal of trouble with this.

"Margaret, it's all right to play this game. Really. Just say whatever I say. Say, 'Uncle Julio, let me go so I can eat.'"

She continued to struggle and it took quite a bit of coaxing before she finally said it, in a tiny, barely audible whisper. "UNCLE JULIO, LET ME GO SO I CAN EAT." Her voice faded out at the end.

"Yeah, but you have to say everything louder than I say it or else I'll win. I'm going to go again. Okay? Uncle Julio, let me go so I can eat."

"UNCLE JULIO, LET ME GO SO I CAN EAT." Her whisper was a bit louder than the first time.

"Margaret, I'm winning the game. You're supposed to say it louder than me." She started giggling and I continued in a silly, exasperated tone. "The one who wins the game is the one who can scream the loudest! Uncle Julio, let me go so I can eat!" My voice rose in volume at the end, making her giggle even more. "Your turn."

"UNCLE JULIO, LET ME GO SO I CAN EAT." Although not by any means forceful, it was closer to her normal-speaking volume.

"That's right. It's just a game. Uncle Julio, let me go *so I can eat!*" I upped the ante.

"UNCLE JULIO, LET ME GO SO I CAN EAT," she responded.

I started saying it faster and faster, louder and louder, and Margaret did the same. Gradually, she began to let go and the pitch of her voice rose beyond what she previously believed to be the limit. It was startling to watch her come to life, going further and further, the energy building until ultimately we both ended up in a screaming frenzy, a cacophony of "Uncle Julios" filling the room.

"UNCLE JULIO, LET ME GO SO I CAN EAT!"

"UNCLE JULIO, LET ME GO SO I CAN EAT!"

And then finally we became one voice, blasting out at full bore, "UNCLE JULIO, LET ME GO SO I CAN EAT! UNCLE JULIO, LET ME GO SO I CAN EAT!"

I wasn't certain if she actually knew what she was saying but she was screaming at the top of her lungs as though she did. "UNCLE JULIO, LET ME GO SO I CAN EAT!"

She began to laugh uncontrollably and shout even louder. But something had changed in the timber of her inflection; Margaret was not laughing out of joy, she was hysterical and in a state of total rage. "UNCLE JULIO, LET ME GO SO I CAN EAT!"

The more Margaret was able to get in touch with her full body empowerment, and leave behind the complacent child who always said "yes" to gain the love of adults, the closer she was to her own source of self. **"UNCLE JULIO, LET ME GO SO I CAN EAT!"** She had never allowed herself this level of freedom before and, impressed by the power of her own wails, screamed all the harder, waving her tiny fists through the air. **"UNCLE JULIO, LET ME GO SO I CAN EAT!"** Her whole body shook with a deep, infectious, purifying laughter. Lost in fits of uncontrolled shrieks, the anger and rage erupted out of her. Her face lit up, her eyes opened wide, and from the very depths of her being, as loud as she could, she let out one final scream. The room shook with the sound of Margaret's voice and then with the silence that follows an explosion.

I looked at her and saw she was embarrassed and not sure what to do. "It's okay, sweetheart, that was just about the best scream I ever heard."

A rosiness I had never seen before caressed her face. The place of darkness was now an open space and, where once blocked, her energy now flowed. The force of her will to live had carried out the darkness that once held her hostage. The anomaly was gone. She was free. Slowly, I helped her fill the newly vacant area with the essence of herself so that nothing else could take up residence in the space formerly occupied by Uncle Julio's negative intent. She was now one hundred percent the bright light known as Margaret, her core so unique, no other star in the vastness of the universe could shine in quite the same manner.

When it was over we were both exhausted, but whatever it was, it was done. Margaret had a renewed sense of her own power and now the empty place in her was filled with herself; there was no longer a void for Uncle Julio to fill. He was unable to get a grip on her even when she was outside of my field.

Julio was still in the room though, standing to the right side of the table. The connection from her third chakra to his fist appeared to be transformed; it was still there but it was no longer dark. It was clean and clear, Margaret's aura bright and full.

As my anger subsided, I began to wonder about this man, this lost soul named Julio. What pain had he gone through in his life? What caused the distortion that compelled him to have an unhealthy relationship with a child—a relationship so strong it transcended the grave? Any soul that was still hanging on to something or someone this desperately, rather than growing and evolving, deserves love. There was nothing wrong with his knowing that Margaret loved him, and it was all right for him to go on loving her as well. But he needed to learn about healthy relationships and I was not to be his teacher.

Julio, walk into the light. It is the light of our Lord. Please, Uncle Julio, peace awaits you. Almost instantly, he started moving toward the Holy presence.

As he drifted across the room, I wondered whose soul had actually been saved that day. Although I believed I was there strictly for Margaret's sake, watching as this deeply troubled individual was enveloped in the image of love gave me cause to reconsider. Perhaps it was not so simple. In the next moment, Julio and the Light were indivisible. An instant later, they were gone.[2]

Margaret was still on the table and just starting to catch her breath, occasionally hiccuping a laugh or two.

"That was a lot of fun, wasn't it?" I asked.

"Yeah, that was a lot of fun. Did I win?"

"Can't you tell? You certainly yelled louder than I did."

I quickly completed what was left of my work and, as I was helping her off the table, casually asked if she loved Jesus. She said yes.

"Well, be sure to include him in your prayers. And don't always just ask him for his help. Every once in a while, thank him for just being there. I think that's a good thing to do."

She just giggled.

"I don't imagine I'll see you again before Christmas, but you can call or come by whenever you feel like it. I'd love to hear from you. We have an appointment for the thirtieth, so I'll see you then for sure." The session over, we went to get her mother.

In the parking lot, Teresa looked at me through pleading eyes and then turned to Margaret and asked, "How'd it go?"

Her response, on the heels of what had just transpired, caught me completely off guard. Margaret said, "She's silly, that's all."

As they got into the car, I looked her over one last time and said, "I hope you get what you want for Christmas."

"Me too," was her reply.

At the last moment, just as Teresa was about to close the car door, I blurted out, "Hey Maggie, whatever you do tonight, don't eat pizza! No pizza. No way. Got it?" I was aware that pizza was her favorite food, but I don't know what possessed me to make such a horribly inappropriate comment.

By the look on her face, Teresa was wondering the same thing. Margaret, on the other hand, thought this was the funniest thing she'd ever heard and laughed her little head off.

It felt like a huge event had taken place, but there seemed little point in talking to Teresa about it. There was nothing to confirm that the session had made any difference; there was no proof or physical evidence. Energy techniques, spinning chakras, visions, and psychological concepts were not what really made the difference. What mattered was Margaret— her pain, her laughter, her connection to whom she loved and what she believed in, including her Uncle Julio. No technique, traditional or otherwise, could come close to the power of Margaret's own faith . . . and it only took one person to notice and confirm that faith for its power to be released— "Wherever two or more are gathered . . ."

I didn't test Margaret with the candy cane to see if she could swallow while outside my field. But she seemed so happy when she left, the way she skipped to the car.

9

That night, around eight-thirty, the phone rang and on the other end was a little girl's voice. "Roseanne?"

I assumed it was my six-year-old niece and said, "Oh, hi, Lindsay, how are you?"

"No, it's not Lindsay, it's Margaret," the small voice said. The world stopped spinning.

"Hi, Margaret. What's up? I didn't expect to hear from you so soon."

"I have something to tell you."

"What is it?"

"Guess what I did tonight?"

"I don't know, what did you do?"

"I ate pizza. Two pieces."

In that moment I was sure the world was made of honey and nectar. "Pizza? I thought I told you not to have pizza. I know I told you not to have pizza! You must not have been listening to me! I'm sure I said no pizza!"

Margaret laughed and said, "You know what else I did?"

"No, what else?"

"I ate bread."

In a voice of mock admonishment, I asked, "Well, young lady, is there anything else you want to tell me?"

"Yes. I had Brie cheese."

"Br-rie! Well my, my, my, aren't we getting fancy. Anything else?"

She meticulously listed every morsel she had eaten and I dutifully reacted with outrage to her delight. Then Teresa got on the line.

"You just wouldn't believe it, Roseanne. She ate nearly half a pound of cheese and half a loaf of bread! And then all that pizza!"

"Teresa, I can't tell you how happy this makes me, but I'm a little concerned about her digestion. It would have been better to start her out on mashed potatoes, broth, or something light."

"Roseanne, we got home, I started to make dinner, and for the first time in over two months Margaret said she was hungry. I asked her what she wanted to eat and she said pizza. When your little girl hasn't eaten in two months, you give her anything she wants. So we ran out and bought a pizza."

"All right, it's wonderful. I agree. But, if she has a stomachache tonight, call me."

"Don't worry, Roseanne, everything is going to be okay now."

I knew she was right. Something I had secretly been hoping for had taken place, but my contribution lay largely in surrendering to a greater energy, not fighting it, and not trying to figure it out. Perhaps a truth this humble is not inglorious.

I had a great Christmas. A marvelous dinner.

10

This time, when the van pulled up, I ran to it without inhibition and didn't slow down until Margaret was in my arms hugging me.

"I love you," I told her.

She said, "I love you, too."

It was the last time I was to see her, and although I knew this visit wasn't strictly necessary, I welcomed the opportunity to be with her again, to say good-bye. Teresa was working and couldn't make it, so Margaret's father, Mark, brought her to the office this time. He also brought her younger sister—the child I had known Teresa was pregnant with when we worked together.

I held Margaret in my arms and immediately knew how well she was doing. It was apparent her field was maintaining its clarity and balance; there was no darkness, no issue of invasion, no sign of an unhealthy connection to Uncle Julio. We sat down and for no apparent reason began to laugh. Once again, there was an opening within me, the feeling as if I was actually expanding. And in that fullness I could feel Margaret and was enveloped by the youth and exuberance of a six-year-old. It was intoxicating. She was so much fuller than when I first saw her; I knew this was a precursor to health. The dark circles under her eyes were completely gone. She was in great shape and so full of energy, she could barely sit still.

"So, what did you get for Christmas?"

She told me about the gifts she'd received as she fidgeted with the drawstrings of her coat. She never once mentioned food or eating; the subject was already obsolete and no longer of concern. I performed a quick "chelation" in between Margaret's constant interruptions. It was essential she tell me about her best friend and the recent snow. She was much more interested in sledding conditions than in what I was doing. Before she hopped off the table, I took one final look around for Uncle Julio. He was nowhere to be found.

The session only lasted about half an hour, but it was reassuring to meet Mark, although I could feel his discomfort with whomever or whatever he thought I was. He never asked me to explain what had happened in the previous sessions but was clearly happy his daughter was eating again. He seemed like a good man, a good father. He was attentive and quietly protective of both his daughters, and his concern for them was comforting. His presence brought a solidity to this family and his girls obviously adored him.

I told Margaret she was doing great and she readily agreed. She finished filling me in about her latest school adventures and what she thought of her new teacher—small talk between friends. Right before she left, she mentioned Christmas dinner, just a passing comment, no big deal, good food, good fun, and good family, everything normal. *Normal.* What a beautiful word.

After one final hug in the parking lot, she got in the van with her father and sister and drove away.

A few days later, there was a knock on my office door. It was unusual for someone to ignore my "Do Not Disturb" sign and I couldn't imagine who it was. In the late afternoon darkness stood a man with a vase of long-stem red roses. It had been a very long time since anyone had sent me flowers. I took them inside, searching every corner of my mind trying to figure out who they might have come from.

I was surprised by the intensity of my longing for them to be from some secret admirer. Memories of every recent acquaintance raced through my mind. *Who could it be?* I wondered, fanning the flame of the impossible hope, the salvation of a new love. I sat on the couch and excitedly removed the envelope from the arrangement.

I broke the seal and took out the card. There were just three words and a signature on it. My disappointment was only momentary as the words sank in: "I love you. Margaret."

I thought: typical of Teresa, always so considerate and sweet. I waited until I was sure she was home from work before calling to thank her.

"Well," Teresa responded, "I don't know what you did—Margaret said you say and do funny things—but whatever it was, it worked and we're very grateful. But the roses aren't from me, they're from Margaret."

"I know, I know," I said just to be polite.

"Really, Roseanne. It was her idea. I think she knows we didn't pay you because she was very concerned we get you a gift. We asked her what and she suggested roses. I hope you like them."

"I do. Very much," I said, recalling Great-Grandma Rose's message: *Fresh cut flowers . . . good for the soul.*

Since then, I've spoken to Teresa only upon occasion. Generally very short, quick conversations, usually around the holidays. "We're happy, things are great, Margaret's fine."

Years have passed and Margaret is at least eleven or twelve by now. I haven't seen her since that last office visit, although I called recently to find out how things were going. Teresa said she was perfectly fine, eating well, fighting with her sister, growing up. Everything normal.

"Tell her I said hello," I said and then quickly added, "She probably doesn't remember me."

"Oh, yes, she does," Teresa corrected me. "She mentions you from time to time. She'll be really excited when I tell her who's on the phone. Hold on, I'll go get her."

I held on.

PART TWO

Charity

Marissa

11

When I was just a little girl
I asked my mother what would I be?
Would I be pretty?
Would I be rich?
Heres what she said to me
Que sera sera
Whatever will be, will be
The futures not ours to see
Que sera sera
What will be, will be.

Whatever Will Be, Will Be
(Que Sera, Sera), words and music
by Jay Livingston and Ray Evans

Ann Marie also worked with Teresa; they were friends. That's how she got my number. It was the first week of November and she called shortly after my prayer for the holiday season, the moment I had chosen at random that was now a yearly ritual, a ritual inspired by Amanda and manifest in Margaret. I was not at all surprised at how quickly the phone responded this time, although experience had done little to lessen the knee-jerk fear. Perhaps I was even more frightened than before, but I answered the phone after just one ring.

"This is Roseanne."

"Hello, my name is Ann Marie," she began in a soft, steady voice. She said she'd been working with Teresa for the past several years and was calling at her suggestion. "I don't really understand what it is you do, I don't even know if Teresa actually understands what you do, but she said you saved her daughter's life."

"Well, that's very kind of her but a bit of an overstatement. How can I help you?"

"I have a three-year-old daughter; she's going to be four in January. Her name is Marissa. She's been having a series of hysterical fits, sometimes crying uncontrollably for as long as eight straight hours. It happens for no apparent reason, and no one can seem to figure out why. Teresa said you might be able to help us."

"It must be difficult for her to sleep," I said automatically. I was not avoiding her last comment, but I was in a state of disbelief that my annual prayer had again been answered with another little girl.

"She sleeps very little and usually wakes up in the middle of the night, screaming. Once she gets hysterical, there's absolutely no way to calm her down. You have no idea how difficult it is to live with a screaming child day in and day out. I've never seen anything like it. We're all at our wit's end. There's no reason for her to act this way and it's beginning to drive my husband crazy—we also have an infant, which makes the situation even more difficult."

"What do the doctors say?"

"They don't know what's causing this. There doesn't seem to be anything physically wrong; she's not in any kind of physical pain or anything like that. They gave us some advice but none of it has had any effect. What frightens me most is how suddenly these fits appear. One moment she's fine and the next, totally hysterical."

"Is she high-strung or particularly sensitive?"

"Everyone agrees that this isn't some sort of tantrum on her part. When it's happening, nothing and no one can comfort her. This is genuine hysteria. There's something terribly wrong. I'm frightened, my husband is frustrated, and Marissa is miserable, barely able to function. I feel like my family and my life are falling apart. Can I bring Marissa to see you?"

"Of course. When can you come in?"

"Oh, let me see. I'll check my calendar."

12

There were no openings in my schedule, so I arranged to see Ann Marie and Marissa early one morning before the day's patients began to arrive. I watched from the doorway as they got out of the car and crossed the parking lot. It struck me that Marissa didn't appear to be the totally out-of-control, hysterical child Ann Marie had described on the phone. Not at all.

What I saw was a delicate, seemingly shy, possibly depressed little girl with exceptionally dark circles under her eyes. She looked weary, but what really struck me was that she appeared worried, deeply worried. I had never before seen a three-year-old look this way, the weight of the world on her tiny shoulders, her baby face contorted with concern.

They entered the office and Ann Marie introduced us. "Marissa, this is Roseanne. I told you we were coming to see her."

I expected Marissa to recoil from me and cling to her

mother. But I did no more than bend down, so that we were at eye level to say "hi" and, without a second of hesitation, she put her arms around my neck and held on as I stood back up. It was like holding no weight at all—her sweetness lighter than air. I asked her where she'd like to sit but she wasn't ready to talk and just stayed with me as I sat on the couch.

Ann Marie looked strikingly similar to Margaret's mother, Teresa. In fact, if you put them side by side, you'd think they were sisters. There were also similarities in their demeanors, although it was my impression that Teresa was a little tougher underneath. Ann Marie, in contrast, seemed more submissive: her head down, her voice never exceeding soft-spoken. It was easy to see she had reached the end of her rope; her kind, round face was lined with worry.

I mouthed to her over Marissa's shoulder, "Does she always go so easily to strangers? Is this normal for her?"

"No, not at all. In fact, quite the opposite."

I gently bounced Marissa while Ann Marie completed the intake form. She had written relatively little information on it but, significantly, under "reason for visit" she wrote: "Marissa was molested by her uncle. She has nightmares and is very, very out of control. She will cry for absolutely no reason. Please help her to be able to deal with what's going on in her world." She hadn't mentioned the molestation on the phone.

Marissa slipped from my lap and quietly went to sit at her mother's side. I caught her eye and we smiled at each other. There was a delicacy about her that was at once both disarming and breathtaking. In many ways she reminded me of a bird: exquisite, graceful, fine. But she was also dark, exotic, and full of vinegar. She had straight black hair, a clear olive complexion, and two large black almonds for eyes—a perfect porcelain doll come to life.

I put the intake form aside, the one sentence still working its way through me. Although I was unable to ask Ann Marie questions in a direct way, I was able to gather she didn't know the extent of the molestation or exactly what had happened. I decided, if it was necessary, I could call her later for the details.

Since Marissa seemed to be comfortable with me, I immediately began to work with her. I gave her Bear, as I had with Amanda and Margaret, and told her I wanted her to do to him whatever I did to her. She took the white bear by its red scarf and started dragging him away. As the scarf tightened around Bear's neck, I spontaneously started making choking noises as though I were the one being choked. In a funny, gagging voice I acted out the part of Bear: *Marissa, you're choking me!* She immediately understood and pulled the scarf tighter around Bear's neck, choking him with more enthusiasm, laughing her head off all the while.

Our rapport was natural and spontaneous; the more I coughed and gagged, the tighter she pulled the scarf. After several minutes of this, I took Bear from her and held him in front of my face. Seriously shaking him, I said in full voice, "Don't do that to me!" Marissa took Bear back from me and began to shake him, too. Then she started punching him, then throwing him on the floor, then stomping him. It was getting quite violent and I did everything I could to aid in the process. I picked him up and threw him in her direction as hard as I could, careful not to hit her. She winged him back at me. The exchange became more and more physical as we threw Bear back and forth, harder and harder.

I could see Ann Marie out of the corner of my eye. Moments before, she was ready to burst into tears at the sight of her daughter's tenderness in my arms. And then suddenly, and for no apparent reason, I had turned that sweet gentility into the raging sumo wrestler that was presently writhing out of control in the middle of the room.

"Don't do that, Marissa. That's not nice," Ann Marie spoke up.

Very gently, I touched Ann Marie on the knee and whispered, "Don't worry, it's all right."

But the intensity was beyond Ann Marie's comfort level and she couldn't help but speak up. "Be careful, you're going to break something," she chided her daughter.

"It's okay," I said.

"Watch out, you're going to knock over that little table."

"It's not a problem. I'm watching her, Ann Marie."

"You're going to break something or hurt yourself."

"Really, it's all right."

I didn't want Ann Marie to feel I was supplanting her motherly authority, but at the same time I needed Marissa to feel uninhibited.

Whereas Margaret struggled to find the energy to scream at Uncle Julio, Marissa had no such trouble finding the emotion to throw Bear at me full force and then altogether pummel him upon his return. She was fully energized and I was constantly concerned she might hurt herself; occasionally, I'd have to shift her location with an errant throw, or get between her and an obstacle.

But for Marissa it was all laughter as she tried her best to annihilate Bear—not the touching laugh of a child, but one laden with pain. She would periodically look to her mom for approval or instructions, to see if whatever she was doing was okay or whether it was time to stop. I did the best I could to make sure Ann Marie didn't give her any cues.

Marissa stepped on Bear's belly before finally plopping to the floor herself, a foot firmly planted across the neck of the vanquished adversary. I asked if she'd had enough and she said yes.

"Are you having fun?"

"Yes, I am," was her out-of-breath response as she crawled back onto my lap.

I gave her Bear and told her to look at him. "Do you have anything to say to Bear?"

She sang a long drawn out "nooooo," the melody admonishing the foolishness of the inquiry. "Bears don't talk."

"You could talk to him if you want."

"Noooo," she said, again singing a similar tune.

With time running short, I asked if she'd lie on my table and she said yes. I helped her up and when she was lying down, I handed Bear to her again. Although I had not consciously recognized what I had seen when she first entered the office, now that she was on the table it was impossible to miss. She was extremely pale, as if shrouded in a dense veil of fog. I was concerned because that darkness, however ethereal, should not have been there.

As with Margaret, I began at Marissa's feet and worked up her body. It was as though I was playing with smoke coming off the tip of a candle; I gently kept brushing it away.

"I want you to do to Bear whatever I do to you, okay?"

"Okay."

"And say to Bear whatever I say to you."

"Okay."

I ran my hands above Marissa's little body and continued to brush away the darkness. She flatly refused to do to Bear what I was doing to her, and I decided to try another approach.

"Marissa, I want you to close your eyes and make a wish."

She lay still, quiet, eyes open.

"Now tell Bear what you wished," I stubbornly pressed on.

She just giggled. There was no way she was going to tell this bear anything. The whole idea was too outrageous to even consider. She just kept holding him tight, eyes open wide, about to burst out laughing.

"Bear wants to know what you wished," I repeated.

She continued giggling.

"What's so funny?" I asked.

"You're funny," Marissa said. "People don't talk to bears." The harder she tried to hold back the laughter, the worse it got. I don't know how it happened, but before I knew it we were both rolling, out of control. The harder we laughed, the better we felt. For the moment, there was nothing more to do. I had the uplifting sense that this moment wasn't just created, it was realized, and we were lost to it, not only connected to each other, but to all things, all possibilities. It was more than just laughter; it was communion.

The sound of our laughter, like music, filled the room and began to rise toward the ceiling, bursting like bubbles in the air. Stardust, perhaps fairy dust, began to rain from the silent explosions.

I was thinking "what could be better than this?" when I noticed Marissa's skin was no longer gray. Her pale cheeks were now luminous, her eyes bright. Marissa continued to giggle away, Bear in hand, a little doll holding a littler doll.

Ann Marie, who'd been sitting quietly all this while, wasn't sure what to make of our giddy hysterics. She looked at me a long moment before speaking. "I haven't seen her smile in months." She turned to Marissa and said, "It's so good to see my baby smile again."

I told Ann Marie I needed to see Marissa again and, without much difficulty, we were able to find a mutually convenient date for the appointment: the twenty-third of December, thirteen days away.

The session was over, and Marissa put her arms fully around my neck and hugged and kissed me. Clearly, she was happy.

"I love you so much, Marissa. You've got the best smile in the whole world." And I meant it. This couldn't be the child that had been described to me as depressed and disturbed.

"I love you, too," she said and bounded into the car.

After they left, I stood an extra moment in the driveway before returning to the office. The opportunity to discuss the abuse and Marissa's uncle never presented itself.

Hoping for some answers, I called that night.

"Hi, Ann Marie, it's Roseanne. I just called to see how Marissa was doing and to discuss any relevant details we weren't able to get to today."

"Oh, I can't talk now, but she's doing great," she assured me in a hushed voice. "She hasn't cried since she left your office. Been in a great mood. Everything's fine. Really, thank you so much."

"I thought it'd be good if we talked; there are some important issues concerning your daughter's condition. I have questions about . . ."

"It's really not a good time for me."

"Well, when can . . ."

"I'm just so busy these days."

"The reason I . . ."

"I know," she said, brushing me off, "I'll see you at the next visit and we can talk then. Is that all right?"

"Sure," I said. There was no point in pressing; Ann Marie already sounded pressured, and there was something disturbing about that—but apparently Marissa was doing well. We said a quick good-bye and I came away with the sense that it was I who wanted to further discuss Marissa's situation, and I who wanted to delve deeper into things, not Ann Marie. Despite being deeply concerned about her daughter, she clearly didn't feel comfortable or safe going into the details that surrounded, and possibly precipitated, Marissa's condition.

13

Marissa had a relapse exactly one week after their first visit and the hysterical fits returned full force. Ann Marie appeared even more distraught and Marissa again looked tired and worried as she got out of the car. Yet as soon as our eyes met, Marissa's persona seemed to come back to life and she ran right into my arms.

Ann Marie said, "I haven't seen her like this in days. She's actually gotten worse than she was before."

It was my impression Ann Marie thought the first visit may have exacerbated her daughter's condition. Nonetheless, I assumed the shift in Marissa's behavior was likely the result of the natural fluctuations in her energy.[1] I assured her we were making progress but didn't try to explain the psychodynamics of Marissa's energy field, experience having taught me that explanations of this nature would be superfluous to a concerned mother.

Trying not to cry, Ann Marie told me about the strain this was putting on her marriage, how her husband was increasingly losing patience with the situation. Although I didn't say so, her fears concerning the stability of her marriage seemed well-founded. This attempt to help her daughter needed to be a family effort. Instead, here was Ann Marie, alone and hesitant, an exhausted mother fighting to hold the line against whoever or whatever was intimidating her.

I thought it might be helpful to at least include her husband in the process and told her I would be happy to talk with him, but she made it clear he was fervently unwilling to work with us. Just the same, I tried to impart the information he needed, knowing it was unlikely any of it would reach him.

Through the distraction of unspoken truths and buried emotions, I tried to figure out what might have caused Marissa's relapse. I still hadn't had the opportunity to confer with Ann Marie privately. The night I called, she sounded guarded and uncomfortable, as though she might be overheard, a sense of fear and secrecy betraying her carefully chosen words.

Marissa and I connected in very much the same manner as we had the first session. We played with Bear and she acted out with him just as violently as she had before, throwing him around and punching him. What she enjoyed most, though, was throwing him at me as hard as she could. I wasn't sure

Ann Marie noticed, but Marissa was hitting, kicking, and throwing Bear with increased intent. This was clearly not a child at play.

I encouraged Marissa as she pummeled Bear and this time I fully participated, rolling on the floor and allowing the session to get even more physical. There was no indication her anger was ever directed at her uncle or anyone in particular, but she had inexhaustible energy for the task.

I said, "Here, take that," and threw Bear at her.

She howled and threw him right back at me.

"Take that and that and this," I said as I hit him and yanked on his ear.

Marissa pulled him out of my arms. She had to one-up me.

"I can hit him harder than you!"

"Bet you can't!"

"Oh yes, I can."

"No, you can't."

"Yes, I can!!!" she roared and feverishly attacked Bear with punch after punch until, red-faced and sweaty, she flopped on the floor and proclaimed, "I win!"

I could feel my heart pounding as Marissa crawled back onto my lap. She looked up at me, smiled, slumped down, and released an immense sigh. I felt her shoulder melt into my chest and her arms slip around me. She closed her eyes.

The session was nearly at its end, and I spent the final minutes pondering the connection between Marissa and her uncle. I realized I knew nothing about this man who obviously had a devastating effect upon this child. Who was he? Where was he? How often did Marissa see him? What happened?

What I knew, in the here and now, was that Marissa was again shrouded in the gray mist and had several anomalies inhibiting her first, second, and third chakras. I attended to them quietly so as not to disturb her. Chakras, when functioning well, are bright "wheels of light" as Rosayln Bruyere calls them. Marissa's looked more like faded, lopsided pinwheels. As before, as always, I could only hope my brief intervention would have a lasting effect.

This time when Ann Marie tried to put Marissa in the car, she held on to me and didn't want to go. "Can I come back?" she asked. "Please?"

"Of course, you can," I assured her, having already made another appointment with her mother.

After Marissa was in the car and out of earshot, Ann Marie whispered, "Do you think she'll continue to have episodes? Because I don't know if my marriage can handle it. I mean, my mother and husband just don't understand."

I tried to be as clear, yet as kind, as I could. "Everyone in the house needs to understand that what happened to your daughter is having a profound effect on her, and the way you handle this situation, as a family, is just as important as anything I can do here." She wasn't comforted by this, but I went on. "I definitely feel that these sessions have been helpful, but I don't think the work with Marissa will hold unless the whole family is involved with her healing."

I paused and waited for Ann Marie's response. "Go on," she whispered.

"I realize this kind of situation puts a great deal of pressure on a marriage. God knows it must be stressful having a child who has unprovoked, unpredictable fits of hysteria, but you need some space for your own sanity, a place to relax and let go. I think it would be good if you had someone to talk to, too. It might help. And if you, or any other member of your family, should ever want to see me here or talk to me on the phone, you're certainly welcome to do that."

Before they left, I embraced Ann Marie and she hugged me back, but only a little. I told her we'd talk some more at the next appointment and reminded her she could call any time. As they drove away Marissa turned around and waved until the car was out of sight.

14

Ann Marie called a few days later to tell me how well things were going. She said Marissa was like a completely new child. "The news couldn't be better except there is one small thing."

"What's that?"

"Well, Marissa's got something in her head and she just won't stop bugging me about it. She brings it up everyday."

"What is it?"

"She wants a picture of you. Actually, she wants a picture of you and her together. Would you mind terribly if we brought a camera to the next appointment?"

"Not at all. Can I talk to Marissa?"

"Sure, I'll get her."

A few seconds later, Marissa picked up the phone, "Hello."

"I heard you want a picture of you and me together."

"Yes."

"That would be great. We'll do it on your next visit."

"Promise?"

"I promise. I love you, you know."

"I love you, too," she giggled.

Her request for physical proof of our relationship flattered and melted me on the one hand, and struck me as somewhat ominous on the other—as though Marissa was looking to take some part of me with her so she could hold onto the feeling she had in the office. I wanted to hold onto that feeling too. With a few simple giggles, we had reached into each other and created an inexplicable bond. Whatever it was she received from our sessions needed to be consistently available to her at home—and it wasn't so much about me, or what I did, as it was about what I represented. Considering the tension of the previous phone call, her request only served to reinforce my speculations about her tender state of vulnerability and her need for protection.

No child, certainly not Marissa, has the perfect childhood. Although impacted by the abuse, like everyone else, she was also profoundly affected by the overall care she was receiving. When she was grown, she would most likely forget the everyday, normal, unsensational goodness of being cared for and loved, remembering mainly the good times and the bad. Most of her childhood, indeed most of her life, would blend neatly and unnoticed into itself, into a real fairy tale.

In proportion to the span of a lifetime, no technique, or office visit or practitioner, or pill, or surgery, or therapy of any kind can replace the security of a family's love and care—not in Marissa's life or anybody else's. It's not the intervention or the one magical moment that matters, it's the every moment. The high and low points, the anomalies, although memorable, are rarities, exceptions. They are just roadside markers to remind us of where we are in our lives, indicators of what we are learning, not the blueprint of who we really are.

It's also possible that most of the emptiness in life, most of the desolation and depression, stems from the erroneous belief that God is here for the highs but not the lows, and is nowhere to be found when we need answers, when we need support, and especially when we don't believe. The truth must be that Spirit is present all the time, meeting us one hundred percent, no matter what, even if a child has been molested, even if a mother is struggling to hold a family together, even if I can't find a way to help either of them. God must be present, even if it makes no sense, even if there is no proof.

15

Tired of stretching, I walked down a cobblestone road and found a seat on the foundation of a house that no longer needed support. Several runners came by and struck up conversations, pretty much the usual: Do you know this course? Is it tough? Any hills? Run any races lately? Since I didn't know the course and it had been a year since my last competition, I mostly listened as people spoke of strategies and training routines. Some were anxious, others hopeful. I just wished the race would start—which I suppose put me in the anxious category.

Before leaving for the race, I'd stopped at my office to check my messages, hoping there would be one from Ann Marie. There wasn't. The last time she called it was to say she couldn't keep the appointment because she wasn't able to get out of work. She asked if her husband could bring Marissa and I told her that would be fine, great in fact; I wanted to meet him.

When she called again, it was to tell me her husband was having car trouble and they wouldn't be coming at all. Ann Marie said it was all right because the crisis had passed; Marissa was laughing again and sleeping peacefully through the nights. No more fits. But there was something troubling about a few hours of missed work or car trouble taking precedence over their child. And it was more than that. It was as though the work was incomplete. Although overjoyed by Marissa's apparent recovery, something was still missing, and I was certain she should return for a closure session at the very least.

I made every suggestion I could think of, changing my schedule every which way to accommodate them. Yet the more solutions I came up with, the more resistance I encountered. There had to be something going on in their lives that I wasn't privy to. I stopped pushing, not wanting to provoke a further shutdown.

I called Ann Marie three times after that, at work and at home, but always got an answering machine. I left messages saying, "I would still like to see Marissa. If you'd rather not have an appointment, just give me a call and let me know how she's doing all the same." I still hadn't heard from her.

The 5K race began in the parking lot of the hospital that was sponsoring the event and crossed the grounds of what had once been the Rockefeller estate. I arrived alone and registered early, which made the forty-five minute delay feel even longer than it was. When the gun finally went off, the runners poured out of the parking lot and headed down the cobblestone road that ran past the remains of what once was a stately mansion. Seconds later, the trail turned sharply downhill and we entered a wooded area that ran along the Hudson River. I knew I was moving at a faster pace than normal, not by much, but enough to notice. I chalked it up to the excitement of the event.

It took nearly a mile for the pack to spread out and I was alone as I left the woods and started across a long stretch of open field. The sun was hot and I was already starting to sweat when I heard footsteps behind me, so close I could hear whoever it was breathing. Making no effort to pass, the runner stayed on my heels without speeding up or slowing down, matching my every step for the next quarter mile. I finally took a quick look over my shoulder and caught a glimpse of a middle-aged woman about five-and-a-half feet tall with curly, almost frizzy, shoulder-length hair. She looked tough and determined and, at the same time, tired and worn.

In an attempt to pull away from her, I sped up for a short distance, hoping to escape the sound of her labored breathing but, huffing and puffing, she pushed to stay with me. It didn't make sense; we were, at best, in the middle of the pack with no hope of winning the race. Why was this woman dogging me? When I couldn't take it any more I moved to the side of the trail, leaving her no choice but to pass. After she went by, I resumed my natural pace, still struggling to run my race. I ran up a slight incline, followed the course into a sharp U-turn, and moments later found myself on top of her again. I passed her effortlessly without altering my pace and when she responded by picking up hers I let her pass again. Over the next mile, I found myself constantly adjusting my speed to compensate for her erratic behavior. If I fell behind, she slowed down; if I sped up, she'd stay on my heels.

As we left the field, the course narrowed considerably, making it difficult to pass, and the woman stayed several steps ahead of me, struggling to hold her lead. I did not want to slow down and I knew sprinting this early in the race was not a good idea. I wanted to put more distance between us but wasn't sure how to do it. Ultimately, in an attempt to get her out of my mind, I began running with my head down, focusing on my feet and counting my steps. This slowed my pace considerably.

I was still looking down when the course changed from dirt to pavement and turned uphill in a long, steady incline. When I checked to see how far the top was, I saw the woman again; although well ahead of me, she had slowed to a walk and by the time I caught up to her was nearly at a standstill, bent over and breathing heavily. I immediately felt bad about having been so agitated by her, realizing I had made her into a projection of something with no idea what she might be up against in life. After all, she wasn't there to ruin my race; she was simply trying to run her own.

I stopped and asked if she was okay.

"Fine," she gasped.

"Come on," I said, "you can do it."

She kept taking deep, difficult breaths, staring at the ground.

"Come on, run with me. I'll pace you."

When she finally looked up, the expression on her face said something stronger than "go to hell" and I instantly understood I had earned it. With a sideways scowl that made it clear she was not in trouble and didn't need my help, the woman straightened up and began to run beside me. In less than half a mile, she had her breath back and was in full stride. At the crest of the hill, I sped up and pulled away, running the rest of the race knowing she was behind me but not sure how far, forcing myself not to turn and look.

The final leg of the race led the runners into a large parking lot that curved around a contemporary office building. A small cloud drifted in front of the sun, cooling the air, and I realized I was beginning to enjoy the race. Leaving the parking lot and entering another wooded area, I finally felt I'd found my inner world and outer pace; a certain tranquility pervaded. Knowing it couldn't be much farther to the finish, I searched for distance markers without success, but it was soon academic. From the edge of the woods I could see that cones had been set up in the hospital parking lot and a finishing lane cordoned off. A large digital clock recorded the times of the runners as they crossed the finish line—a surprisingly official ending for such a small race, I thought.

Having just settled into my stride, I was almost disappointed the race was over and realized, with the slightest regret, that I had plenty of reserve and could have gone considerably faster. As I entered the finishing lane, feeling a bit self-conscious, I decided to use up some of my extra energy and sprint the final yards. I was about to pick up the pace when, from out of nowhere, I heard pounding footsteps and the familiar sound of heavy breathing. Before I could react, I felt the sharp stab of an elbow in my ribs and, in the next instant, the woman I had tried to help up the hill pushed past me. Regaining my balance, I fought the urge to tell her off as I crossed the finish line, one step behind her.

I wasn't relieved the race was over, just angry. I started for the parking lot in no mood to talk to anyone about their times or anything else. Just as I reached my car, one of the runners yelled over to me not to forget my complimentary T-shirt. It's just a stupid T-shirt, I reminded myself as I headed all the way back toward the registration area to get one.

After getting the shirt, I started back through the crowd toward the parking area. By this time, the race organizers had already begun to announce the names of the winners. My attention was on the makeshift stage as the fastest runners went up to collect their medals. When they began to announce the winners of the forty-and-over division, I stopped in my tracks. It never crossed my mind that a race this small would have divisions.

Now it all made sense. The woman knew all along that if she beat me out she would win the division, a division that I had no idea I was in. When they announced my name as the second-place finisher, I made my way to the podium in a state of shock, taking my place next to the first-place medallist as cameras clicked away. With willful control, I turned to the woman who had elbowed her way to victory and congratulated her. She just stared and scowled, so I responded for her, "You're very welcome." She turned and walked away, her husband and children waiting to congratulate her. Medal in hand, I couldn't wait to leave.

It struck me that I had not run my own race; I had allowed this strange woman to affect my pace. It wasn't her I was mad at, it was me. By the time I got home, I had decided not to run in any more races. Eventually the anger subsided into the dull ache of self-reproachment, and my thoughts settled on Ann Marie and what she must be going through. Whereas Teresa had no idea what had occurred with her daughter, Ann Marie knew about a specific incident of abuse and, along with being concerned, had to be furious. Having just experienced the powerful effect anger had on me, I couldn't help but wonder how she was handling hers. I wondered what was on her tail and what adjustments she was making to keep whatever it was from catching up to her—or to keep herself from catching up to it. Of this much I was certain: she'd been hiding the fact from her family that she was bringing her daughter to see me, and this was part of an issue that working with Marissa could not address. I had the feeling Ann Marie was running away from something, and losing her way in the process.

Marissa never got her photograph. Her request now seemed like a prophecy.

16

If needed, an oxygen mask will drop from the compartment above your seat. To start the flow of oxygen, pull the mask towards you. Place it over your nose and mouth and slip the elastic band over your head, tightening the strap as necessary. Always secure your mask first before attempting to help a child or someone else who may need your assistance.

—FAA Flight Regulation

I didn't want to work with Alex, not because of her condition, but because I was sure I was walking into failure. From the sound of Mary's voice on the phone, it was clear she believed she could find a miracle, that someone could come along and wondrously make her child normal. She said, "I believe anything can happen. Doctors can be wrong, things can change." She was determined and unwilling to let anything or anyone kill her hope. Despite this, I agreed to see Alex; she was the answer to my annual prayer. Another year had passed and it was once again autumn. Amanda, Margaret, Marissa, and now Alex. Four years, four little girls.

Mary exuded a kind of togetherness—the set of her jaw, the chiseled features, the piercing eyes, the cut of her hair. Strong. Together. She was the least emotional and most business-like of all the mothers I had worked with so far. In many ways, this made her desperation all the more heartbreaking. She said

Alex had been having seizures for the last eighteen months and that they'd seen regiments of neurologists and psychologists. In addition, she told me her daughter suffered from a series of severe long-term behavioral problems, not the least of which was that she had never learned to speak.

My first thought upon seeing Alex was that I couldn't believe she hadn't been diagnosed as autistic. She was, at best, just slightly more connected than those classically afflicted— but just slightly. Once in awhile I got the feeling she could listen if she wanted to, but it could well have been wishful thinking on my part.

The doctors said her seizures were probably a form of epilepsy, but clearly there were overlapping or simultaneous disorders. In addition to being unable to speak, Alex displayed other traits characteristic of autism: rocking, repetitive motions, an inability to focus or maintain contact. She could stare at a pencil for endlessly long periods of time but could not tolerate more than a few seconds of human interaction. I didn't know what was going on in her world, but epilepsy certainly couldn't explain all of these symptoms.

She was twice as big as Marissa and had long blond hair and graceful, butterfly lashes. Another heartbreaker.

From the moment she entered the office, Alex never stopped moving and never sat down. She'd occasionally try to get something off the table and invariably knock it onto the floor, only to forget about it and walk away. It was necessary to keep a constant eye on her, as she was apt to bump into things or fall down.

"What do you want me to get her to do?" Mary asked.

"She's fine the way she is. Just let her be."

"I could try to get her up on the table, if you like."

"No, this is okay. I'd just like to observe her for awhile."

I would have loved to hold Alex in my arms, but this was all but impossible. She didn't let anyone hold her, not even her mother. I tried putting my hands on the sides of her head to see if I could get some sense of what was going on, but she brushed me away and moved out of range. There was no acknowledgment I was even there beyond whatever fleeting discomfort I might have caused—like a mosquito or a cold rush of air. Sometimes she focused on something unseen, usually looking up and to the right. These were her only periods of stillness and they were extremely intense; I'd swear she was looking at something quite real.

Much of the session consisted of her wandering around the office with me following, attempting to put my hands on her head. I was only able to touch her for a few seconds at a time.

"Are you sure we shouldn't try to get her on the table?" Mary asked.

"No, let's just let her be. Does she ever make eye contact?"

"Rarely. When she does, it's usually very sudden and very brief."

For want of a better idea, it became my goal to get her to look into my eyes; surely that would represent some sort of progress. As far as I could tell, the only entrance into her psyche was through her extraordinarily clear blue eyes. After an exhausting forty-five minutes, I had managed to make eye contact on only three occasions. Each eye contact lasted longer than the preceding one, the first encounter holding just for a moment, the final for several seconds, maybe three. But in those timeless three seconds, we had walked into each other's soul and a connection had been made despite the fact she did not let me know it: no smiles, no laughs, no hugs. Still, I had gotten three seconds and I was going to believe in them, decide they would matter, make the most of them.

In the deepest moment of our connection, what I found surprised me and, in an odd way, comforted me. Alex was actually accepting of the way she was and there was a purpose to it beyond anything I could understand. And although she never made a sound and didn't respond in any way to my suggestions or commands, I had the distinct impression she understood what was happening and knew when someone was beckoning her. I asked Mary if she thought Alex was aware of what was going on around her.

"I don't know. Sometimes I think so, and then other times I don't."

I sat on the floor in the middle of the area Alex was wandering in and said, "Alex, you know you're lovable just the way you are. You're so precious and so very pretty." I said this several times out loud and continued silently: *I love you just the way you are, drooling, staring at the wall, in your body or out. You don't have to change or do anything to be lovable. I love you here and now, as is.*

Of course, this was incredibly easy for me to say after a mere forty-five minutes of her company. If she were my little girl and I had to take her home and care for her twenty-four hours a day, seven days a week, for the rest of my life, it would not have been so easy. The more I looked at Alex, the drool running down her chin and dripping onto her shoe, the more arrogant I felt for saying, "I love you just the way you are." In five minutes she would walk out the door and someone else would clean up her spittle, her diapers; someone else would bring her to daycare where all the other children could talk and laugh and run and jump and play. I wished I could believe she didn't need saving, but it wasn't that way; I was just like Mary, I wanted to intervene. It was all academic, though; as with Amanda, Alex was here for her own reasons and although I wanted to "save" her, she simply didn't want me to.

The visit ended on this note. Not very eventful. No spontaneous cure. Alex was Alex.

At the door, Mary asked, "How do you think it went?"

"I'm not sure this visit had the effect you've been hoping for," I told her. "I did my best to stabilize her, but it's unlikely there will be any noticeable change."

"We came here for a miracle. I didn't know where else to go or what else to do. Should we make another appointment?"

"I'd like to see Alex as often as possible."

"It's difficult for us to make regular visits. Alex doesn't do very well strapped in the car for long periods of time and it took us two and a half hours to get here today. I mean, we'll come, of course. I'll do anything if you think it'll help."

"Maybe bringing her won't be necessary," I said. "I could try to work with her long distance." Although my physical presence seemed to make little or no difference to Alex, I firmly believed in the connection we had forged and was willing to test it over a distance.

"Long distance?" Mary asked. "What does that mean? How does that work?"

It was a simple question about a complex phenomenon. "What grew out of my encounter with Alex will continue to exist whether we are physically together or not," I responded, "much the way love remains even if the one we love is not in the room with us, or has moved away or died. Energy, of a particular frequency, is conducted through human intentionality and transcends time and space. Healing over a distance works just like a cordless phone, no wires or physical connection. All of us can send or receive energy over any distance. We do it all the time."

"Well, I won't pretend to understand," Mary replied politely, "but I would appreciate anything you could do for us. I believe Alex can get well," she reminded me. "I believe in miracles."

I wanted to believe too.

It was difficult for us to have much of a conversation, with Alex constantly needing attention. I stood by, mostly speechless, as Mary danced with her daughter, trying to get her coat on. Without warning, Alex suddenly stopped resisting the sleeves and buttons and burst into a smile, beaming at us, eyes all asparkle. Mary said she occasionally did this.

The magic of Alex's smile lingered long after they left. It had a force all its own. Whereas Marissa's smile was captivating and full of the vim and vigor of life, Alex's smile, while just as bright, was quite different. It was dharma; a blessing, a gift. It was a miracle.

When I called the following day, Mary told me there hadn't been any noticeable change in Alex's condition. I could hear the disappointment in her voice.

"Mary, maybe Alex's healing isn't about her becoming a normal little girl."

"I still want a miracle for her," she said.

It was exactly what I had asked for while working with Amanda, although I was beginning to wonder if in asking for a miracle we weren't, in some sense, disavowing the God that is here now.

"I know you want a perfect, just-like-everybody-else's little girl, but Alex is not like every other little girl. And for some very special reason she chose you for her mother, maybe because you have the capacity to love her, no matter what. Maybe the miracle is that you love Alex exactly the way she is."

I was asking her to believe in what she already had: the ability to love her daughter the way we want God to love us. I could hear Mary get choked up on the other end of the line, and it was a moment before she could respond. "I understand," she said. "Are you still going to work with her?"

"Yes, of course, twice a week if possible. And I'd like to start tonight."

"Thanks, I appreciate it. Tonight would be good. Alex is usually asleep by 8:30."

"I won't call or anything but I'll be working with her around her bedtime for about half an hour. And please understand me, Mary. Want what you want for your daughter, but allow yourself to take joy and pleasure in whatever presents itself. You'll be in my prayers, too."

I reserved every Tuesday and Thursday night for Alex to continue the relationship we had begun in my office, cemented by the communion we made through our eye contact. It was like I told Mary, Alex was Alex, beautiful, lovable—as is. But I didn't notice any change.

Three weeks later, I received a note from Mary: Alex is doing somewhat better. Her previously rare smiles are coming more frequently and, occasionally, they turn into laughter. Fleeting for sure, but laughter all the same. We are delighted by her new giggling.

Alex had her first seizure when she was three and a half years old. The seizures continued relentlessly for eighteen months and then she settled into a twenty-eight day to thirty-day cycle. Mary could predict the onset of an episode to the day. After our first session, Alex entered the longest seizure-free period of her life—145 days. The neurologist had no medical explanation for the improvement and, although pleased, was rightfully reserved in her prognosis.

No matter how well we do our work, no matter how hard we try, no matter how much we want something, no matter how much faith we have, there are certain things we have no control over and certain things that we have to keep letting go of. It's not the hoping and wishing and not the holding on tighter, it's the letting go that heals—a surrender that is non-selective and open to all possibilities, one that does not necessarily manifest in physical healing, but can change the way we experience our lives. As it was with Amanda, so it was with Alex. We had what we had: the joy that comes in a different way, but is not altogether rare.

The love Mary held for Alex was never in question, but to express that love without hoping for a miracle would have been inhuman. There is only so much even a loving mother can endure before the pressure would build: "Do something, stop drooling, sit still, be normal, listen to me, look at me, love me. Just once, say 'mama.'"

On the 146th day, Alex had another seizure. Ninety days later it happened again and then forty-five days after that. Little by little, despite my continuing efforts, the seizures returned.

17

"Alex, you've gotten so big!"

She moved past me as though I wasn't there. Mary had called a few days before and said that Alex was having seizures on a regular basis again, every thirty days. It had been more than two years since I had seen her in person and the news, although not surprising, was disappointing.

Now seven years old, Alex appeared to be the same child in every way other than size. When not fixated on the ruler she found on my desk (which she kept examining as though it were the most fascinating object in the universe, turning it over and over in her hands), she mostly stared off into space. After exhausting the ruler's potential, she pulled a couple of my diplomas from the wall and dropped them on the carpet before moving on. She was still unable to speak.

Mary had brought Alex's special chair with them in the car; it had straps to hold her in place so she could be fed. Mary assured me Alex didn't mind being in it, and offered to bring it in. I declined the offer and, instead, followed Alex around the room, trying to get in step with her illogical orbit. She still walked awkwardly and, as before, I had to intervene whenever she got near the steps or other potentially treacherous areas. Meanwhile, I kept trying to touch her head, hoping to get some sense of what was going on. The effort was largely futile.

Then we played peekaboo for awhile. By quickly removing

my hands from her eyes, I would occasionally make brief eye contact, but nothing special. Mary joined in and we played several times. Alex did grace us with her marvelous smile as well as her full belly laugh, which I hadn't been privy to at our first meeting. The combination was striking, even startling—like the sun coming out after a thunderstorm, bursting through the clouds.

"That's it right there, Mary. She's giving us a blessing. You've got to love her."

"I do. Always have."

Then Alex was on the move again, with me in tow. This time she let me touch her feet for an encouraging period of time, considering we were in constant motion. Sometimes she seemed oblivious to my touch, other times merely tolerant, and periodically it actually felt as if it were all right. For Alex, each was a vastly different experience: when she was oblivious, she wasn't in her body; when tolerant, she knew I was there but couldn't care less. And then there were those rare moments when she knew I was there and actually allowed me in.

But there were things Alex would not let me do. She would not let me touch her head, stroke her hair, or hold her hand. Alex was not like other children. There was a split through her seventh chakra, like a tree that had been struck by lightning, leaving part of her alive and thriving and the rest fractured off. I was curious as to what might cause a condition like this; was it birth trauma, something hereditary, was there some otherworldly pull on her being?

It was my impression that Alex was not fully present. She was beautiful and growing like a normal child, but part of her, the unseen part, the part that could make her eyes sparkle, most of the time was somewhere else.

She would still periodically look up and to the right, focusing on who-knows-what for several seconds, and I knew it would be impossible to pull her attention back to what was here now if I didn't first find out why she was drifting away. I had no idea how Alex would react to having her connection with "reality" and her physical body so drastically altered. At the very least, pulling Alex out of her world and all the way into her physical body would be disconcerting to her.

I had already noticed that the more Mary wanted Alex to be a normal little girl, the greater was Alex's resolution to remain as she was. The more I wanted her to respond to me, the more she focused elsewhere, diminishing the possibility of contact.

She wouldn't let me anywhere near her. When I tried to hold her hand, she pulled it away. If I whispered in her ear, she turned her head. If I stood directly in front of her, blocking her view, she took two or three steps backwards. Whatever I did, she countered.

Alex knew what she wanted, and she made it perfectly clear that if it was interaction I was seeking, I'd have to force her participation. What I had to fight, more than her condition, was my desire to bring her into normalcy, out of her world and into ours.

In the end, I had to accept that my elaborate techniques had little or no effect. The moments of eye contact were the result of just being with her and not trying to change her. The truth, which I was about to ignore, was that the only way to work with Alex was by first accepting her the way she was.

As it was, I put my hands on her feet and gently tried to pull her back into her body. Her reaction was immediate, reflexive, and definitive: she kicked her feet and walked away. I pursued her and tried again. This time she let me touch her feet for maybe three seconds before kicking me away. Clearly she had no interest in this effort; her desire for things to remain as they were was supreme.

It occurred to me that I had no idea what it was like to be in her body. Maybe she vacated it for good reason. Maybe she'd found a better place. Maybe I was just trying to drag her down. After all, Alex seemed fine; it was Mary and I who had issues.

Two years earlier, I had promised to love and respect Alex as she was, no matter what, so what was I doing trying to fix her, to save her? From what? For what? She was clearly determined to maintain her current guarded relationship with the physical; the soul connection we made through the eye contact was the best I was going to do. It wasn't what I wanted, and it certainly wasn't what Mary wanted, but it was unquestionably what Alex wanted.

Alex delivered another one of her devastating smiles, and I simply added, "That's her. That smile is the answer, the miracle, the blessing. Your daughter is what she is. You can't wait for her growth and improvement to make you happy. Your happiness, your acceptance, your gratitude must be now. That is the healing for all of us."

"But it's so hard. It's so damn hard," Mary said.

"I know these are just words, but they're all I have. I know it's not enough."

"I don't know which direction to run in next. Do you think we should continue to seek out other doctors, other practitioners? No one seems to have any answers."

"Continue to do whatever you think will help Alex, whatever feels right, whatever brings you comfort. I'm sorry I haven't been able to help. I'll continue to make my services available to you and Alex but, as you can see, I don't have any answers either."

Nothing eventful happened during the remainder of the visit: no magic moments, no parting of the seas. The yearning for a "cure" was still with Mary as our time together grew short; she was Alex's mother and would remain forever hopeful. So would I. All as it should be.

Since it was difficult for Alex to move quickly, I knew I'd better get them started on their way when I heard my next patient pull into the parking lot. I was extremely pressured that day, moving appointments around and even squeezing one into my lunch hour. "It's time to go, Alex. Time to get your coat on," I said, gently taking the ruler from her and bending to pick up the jelly beans she had thrown all over the floor. Alex didn't react in any way to my coaxing, so I looked to Mary who, for some reason, appeared to be in shock.

"What?" I said.

"Look at her. Look at Alex."

I looked and pretty much saw what I always saw. "Look at what? I'm not sure what I'm supposed to see."

"Look, look! She's sitting on your couch. Alex is sitting on the couch!"

Missing the point entirely, I said, "Come on, Alex, you really have to get going now."

"Roseanne, she's sitting, sitting down by herself—no straps, no special chair! She's never done this before, ever. She never sits down. She never sits still!"

I didn't know how to respond. Could sitting possibly be a miracle? And if so, then how many miracles do I overlook each day?

"She doesn't want to leave," Mary whispered.

Mary certainly knew her daughter. Every time I reminded Alex it was time to go and Mary slid her off the couch, she climbed back on and sat down. It was a struggle to get her into her coat.

As they were leaving, Mary again asked me what I thought and I told her, "In my honest opinion, I don't think Alex is going to be much different than she is right now. But I think there's a good possibility the seizures may lessen in frequency. Search although you might, the miracle you're looking for is already in your arms."

Mary left with a great deal of sadness, much of which lingered behind. The faith healer had failed. Who's to say she was wrong? Not me. If I gave Alex anything at all, it was a brief moment of time and space where she was okay just the way she was. It was all I had.

18

. . . our stories of God reflect our most profound experiences of being met or overlooked, of being taken up and decoded or left unread.

—from "Telling Our Stories of God:
The Contributions of a Psychoanalytic Perspective"
by John McDargh, *Sacred Stories*

The years were coming and going with more than sufficient speed, and I reminded myself that giving at this time of the year and at all times had to include me: it was not about being empty, it was about being full. The babies, the Christmas babies, had taught me this and now surely it was time to move beyond a pleading mother's eyes, beyond "save me," beyond my own emptiness. This year I needed something. So when the moment came for my annual holiday prayer, I included a request that I not be sent another mother and child. I simply didn't have the strength, or maybe the courage. Not another little girl, please.

When I answered the phone, at first I was relieved.

"My name is Irene. You may not remember me, but I was once a student of yours."

"Of course, I remember you. Irene Santangelo, right?"

"Yes, that's right. I realize you know me as a student but I'm also a sister, a Catholic nun."

"I remember that as well."

"I'm at the convent, not far from your office. There's a sister here who has always taken a keen interest in my studies and would very much like to experience your work. The doctors say she's dying of cancer but she believes she's going to survive. My sense of it is that she's, well, pretty sick."

"And you want me to work with her?"

"If you have time and think it's appropriate. Her name is Sister Gloria."

Although I knew, before the phone call, that I would say yes to whomever and whatever it was, this request had taken me by surprise.

"She's in no condition to travel, so I guess you'd have to make a house call, to the convent."

We agreed that I would visit on the day before Thanksgiving. I didn't know whether Irene was asking me to help the sister to live or to die.

19

As soon as I turned into the driveway, I came upon a lovely stone cathedral with several connecting buildings—all very impressive in scale and grace. The road was sloped and curvy and I got a good look at the grounds, which were equally attractive, adorned with statues. As I parked and got out of my car, I felt the same adolescent feeling I always experienced in a religious setting and hoped I had said my prayers well enough the night before.

I was almost a Catholic. I was to be named Roxanne after my father, Rocco. Unfortunately, there was no Saint Roxanne, making it an unacceptable name for baptism. The issue was settled with a definitive word from my mother, Rose; I was named "Roseanne" after her and then readily accepted for baptism. Ironically, it was to be the last time my mother would play by the rules of Catholicism and, miffed at having been coerced into a second choice of names, shortly thereafter she (and we) became Presbyterian. The only time we went to "that other" church was for weddings and funerals.

My mother's first step off the path actually occurred when she was a child, the fateful morning she took her five-cent Sunday service offering and defiantly bought a pickle. Finding a seat under a shady tree, she savored every bite, expecting God to strike her down, waiting to see if what she had been taught was true. She sat there and waited for exactly one hour but the thunder did not rumble and the lightning failed to flash. The only thing that got struck down that day was the credibility of the church.

As for me, I attended Presbyterian services quite regularly while I was growing up, mostly by myself or with my older sister. I sang in the choir, sat up straight, and tried to be an exemplary Christian. After I entered high school, my church attendance began to decrease in direct proportion to my growing interest in boys, cheerleading, dances, and driving lessons. By the time I completed high school, having fun was more important to me than going to church.

To be honest, the church made me nervous. I disliked the notion that there was a correct way to have faith: if you followed the rules you got to Heaven and if you broke them you didn't. I'll likely always be enamored with the romantic elements of Christianity—the story of Jesus, the ceremonies, the sights, sounds, mysteries, the magic, and myth—but there simply can't be only one right way to fall in love with your own life. Ron Roth, author of *The Healing Power of Prayer*, put it rather well when he wrote: "For too long, religion has portrayed a punishing God, lying in wait to throw the wicked into hell for breaking even one of his laws. I want to spread the word that God is on our side."

I wanted to spread the word as well, but my emotions as I entered the ornate building were those of a lost schoolgirl who, feeling the weight of organized religion, was terrified she'd do something wrong. I was surprised to find the lobby had a very masculine feel, more like a school than a convent. I did my best to follow Irene's directions—down the hall, through the doorway, and up the steps—only to end up in an area that was all but deserted.

Eventually a man came along and politely informed me I was in the monastery. He paused and added, "Where the monks live." I left as invisibly as I could and stiffly walked back to my car, feeling very much like I had entered the wrong restroom. Right under God's nose, I couldn't get it right.

The buildings that comprised the convent were not as imposing as those of the monastery. They were constructed of a common red brick and considerably less lavish in style. The facility had the appearance of a nursing home with an attached residence. There was a lovely grotto nestled into the side of the hill which housed a statue of the Virgin Mary. There was no cathedral.

This time I followed the instructions correctly and Irene, who'd been at the window watching, met me in the lobby and led me inside. As we walked down the long, wide corridor, I noticed there were many nuns present, some in full habits, others simply in blue and white headpieces with matching skirts and blouses; some were wearing conservative street clothes, and several were in wheelchairs, apparently patients. But most of them just seemed to be milling around. I didn't think much of it, although it struck me they were not there randomly. Their eyes followed me but their faces betrayed no opinion. I lowered my head and continued down the hall.

The line of nuns ended at a room where two sisters, in full habits, waited on either side of the door. Pausing, I focused inward to prepare myself and in the stillness of the moment realized what all the nuns were here for.

Noticing the look on my face, Irene whispered, "They've come to see you work."

"And this is okay with them?"

"I told them what you do and they want to come in and watch."

"Well, I'd like to meet Sister Gloria first before I commit

to anything. Would you let the sisters know I want to talk with her privately for a few minutes?"

She briefly consulted with one of the nuns and then we entered the room. It was a simple space with little or no adornment. Irene led me to the bed where Sister Gloria lay. She appeared to be in her late sixties or early seventies, very frail with fine white hair.

Struggling up onto an elbow, she exerted herself to welcome me, her eyes bright with hope. I leaned down, touched her arm, and lightly kissed her on the cheek. She was hungry for intimacy and human contact and began explaining her faith to me. I pulled one of the steel chairs as close to the bed as I could and leaned in so she wouldn't have to strain to speak.

She told me that she had been studying the life of an extraordinary saint, the Blessed Josephine Bakhita: Woman of Faith and Forgiveness. It was her unshakable belief that Josephine was going to intervene and save her life. From the table next to the bed, she produced icons of her newly found saint. On one of them was written, "I neither wish to go nor to stay. God knows where to find me when he wants me." Sister Gloria described in detail how and where she had learned about Josephine and told me stories of others who had been saved. The more she heralded her faith, her eminent salvation, the more insistent she became, the more certain I was she was going to die—and relatively soon.

It wasn't a fatalistic vision. It was simply the knowledge that the decision had been made and was flawless. Despite clinging to an image of what a miracle should be, Sister Gloria was already aligned with her death and, although she did not know it consciously, had discovered the glorified being that was her true identity. All she lacked was the cognitive recognition that the love she held for Josephine was precisely the feeling she had for herself. Coming from a sisterhood of humility, I knew she would never speak in this manner, but my job was not to lecture, it was to help make her passage easier.

"How are you, Sister Gloria?"

"Happy," she replied, despite the fear and desperation in her eyes.

"And what is it that makes you so happy, Sister?"

"The love of my blessed saint."

"May I call on her to be with us here today?"

"Oh yes, yes. That's why I wanted you to come. I believe the work you do is similar to hers."

She again began expounding the virtues of Josephine and I grew concerned about time. "Would you like me to work with you?" I inserted at an appropriate moment. "I'd very much like to touch you."

She closed her eyes and with total acquiescence said, "Yes, yes. Oh yes, please do."

She was childlike, willing, and even relieved to put her life in the hands of a stranger, as though she had no say in it at all. At the same time, she exuded the wonder and naiveté of youth. "Yes, I want to live," she was saying, "Touch me, heal me, save me."

I helped reposition her on her back and tried to make her comfortable before moving to the foot of the bed.

"May I touch your feet?"

"Yes, yes."

The instant I touched her, the room filled with the pure silence and luminescence of newly fallen snow. I wondered if her commitment to a spiritual life was, in some way, responsible for so vivid an effect. As I moved up her body and gently touched her limbs, she became emotionally responsive, fully engrossed in her own experience. I touched her ankle and she said "Ahhh," her knee and she said, "Ohhh." For every move I'd make she'd have a reciprocal sigh of pleasure, gratitude, or longing. Her responses were expectant and filled with an anxious need to believe, as if to say "Ahhh yes, the healing is working!" And she was quite right. Although I was not creating the type of physical healing she wanted, I was helping to build a bridge, a bridge intended to unite and return the love she projected, the love she could not directly bestow upon herself, a bridge to the understanding that she could not have recognized the light of Josephine if she did not already possess it.

When I reached her heart chakra, I put both my hands over it, one on top of the other, and waited in silent witness as her spirit connected to the spirit that pervaded the room. I held and solidified the connection, following the divine blueprint that was the architecture of Sister Gloria's life, purposefully making it wider, clearer, and more accessible—unveiling the unification of matter and spirit. We remained in this position for quite some time until I felt energy not only coming down into her, but also emanating out. The connection in place, Sister Gloria could traverse the worlds of physical mortality and spiritual immortality.

I held her face and said, "Your life is fully in your hands. You can live it anyway you want."

Hearing this pleased her very much and I assumed, by her reaction, she interpreted my words to mean she would get well. But I was delivering a much deeper message, one that reconnected her to the personal power and authority that had been lost. Life was here, here now, here for the taking; she could save her own life and die.

I stepped back and realized Irene, who had been sitting quietly to the side all this time, was still there. In silence, I encouraged her to let her own spirit expand along with Sister Gloria's until she was fully integrated into the light and quietude that filled the room. The essences of Christ and the Holy Mother were preeminent and yet the energy was simultaneously all-inclusive; it blended with Sister Gloria and Irene and me, each of us distinct and different, yet radiantly combined, an overwhelming oneness. Unified divinity. Divinely human.

Remembering the sisters in the hallway, I asked Irene if she'd extend my apologies. "I hope I haven't offended anyone.

Would you tell them the healing began spontaneously and I didn't mean to leave them out?"

She assured me no offense would be taken and left the room. I leaned over and whispered to Sister Gloria that it was time for her to sleep. Relaxed from the healing, she closed her eyes and easily fell into a semiconscious state. Lying there, she seemed much the same as when I arrived; the same level of denial and hope, the same sweetness, her body still dying even as her soul awakened.

"The sisters would very much like to thank you for coming." I hadn't heard Irene reenter the room.

"It was my pleasure."

"We would like to show our gratitude in some tangible way," she said.

"No, I won't accept anything for this." We had already discussed this on the phone and it hadn't been difficult explaining to a Sister of Charity why I wasn't charging for the visit.

Ignoring this, Irene picked up a statue of a lion and a lamb from the window sill and offered it to me. "The sisters carve these here at the convent. Would you accept this as token of our appreciation?"

Over my protests, she placed the statue in my hands. It was very nice, obviously an old one, a bit dusty, and apparently not made specifically for my visit.

"This way you'll have part of our life with you," Irene said.

That sealed it for me. "I would love to take part of your sisterhood back with me. I will put it in my office and give it a place of honor."

Sister Gloria, awakened by our conversation, thanked me several more times. I was telling her how welcome she was when she asked, straight out, if I thought the healing had an effect.

"Yes, the healing absolutely had an effect. Sister Josephine was here, the Holy Mother was here, and so was Christ. Did you not feel them bathing you in the golden light, the light of the Divine?"

"Yes, yes, I did," she responded with the glee of a child.

"It had an effect and it will continue. Your life is in your hands; you are the master of your own destiny. Divinity is within you and all around you. God be with you as you know he already is."

The tears ran down her cheeks. "Thank you," she whispered and then closed her eyes and peacefully drifted off to sleep. Moments later I was in the hall, holding the small statue with both hands. I was surprised to discover that nearly all the nuns were still there although the session had taken at least an hour and a half. I walked down the long hall with Irene, feeling the history in the walls, and the sisters, as though magnetized, began to follow. In silence we moved as one, floating, until we arrived at a small chapel and Irene asked if I'd like to go in.

I entered and the sisters did the same. There was a service in progress, apparently for the benefit of the patients in the infirmary, and a priest was at the altar reading from his text.

"Are we disturbing them?" I whispered.

"No, it's okay. They're used to people coming and going during this service."

I sat down with the sisters and gave my attention to the sermon, only to discover that the more I tried to focus on the words the less I heard. Eventually I stopped trying. I wanted what I believed the sisters had: absolute certainty and unwavering devotion. To my left, Irene sat with her eyes closed in reverence, clearly transported. Longing to touch the grace that surrounded me, I shut my eyes to look for God and experienced the comfort of the sister's faith. It was a blessed relief. Some of us need ornate symbols to connect with God, and others just need a hand to hold. I have no idea how much time passed but it was enough. In the house of God I opened my eyes shortly before the liturgy concluded.

I told Irene I needed to get back and she stood to lead the way. As we started down the aisle, the sisters began to reach out: some touching my arm, some shaking my hand, some standing to hug me. "Thank you for having me," was all I could think to say. "I feel honored you asked."

Another round of thanks and Irene and I left the chapel.

"If you have one more minute, there's something I'd like to show you," she said.

She took me to the grotto where the statue of the Virgin Mary stood in grace and beauty, in contrast to the dull surrounding buildings that were the domain of the nuns. I carefully followed in her footsteps, in case there was some ritual concerning one's approach to the Holy Mother. Although I didn't cross myself, I matched the reverence of Irene's nature and stance, and could recall a time when I once believed that if I did everything right and followed all the rules, even if they weren't mine, maybe some good would come of it.

I stood at the foot of the Holy Mother and, despite everything I knew and had learned, wished she would come to life right then and there. I wanted her to step off her pedestal and take me in her arms and hold me. I wanted her to tell me I was lovable and had not been overlooked. In that split second, I again wanted to believe in the smoke and the mirrors, the mysteries and the myth. I told Irene to call if Sister Gloria should ask for me, and we embraced at the feet of the Holy Mother.

A few months later, on Valentine's Day, Irene called to tell me Sister Gloria had died. It seemed well within character for the good sister to choose a saint's day for her passing and equally appropriate that my fervent desire to not be sent another child that year go unheeded. For I was sent a child: a child of God. Could it have been otherwise?

Several months after Gloria's death, Irene came to a lecture I was giving and stood at the back of the room. I didn't notice her until the session was over and she was coming forward with a plainly wrapped package in her hands.

"The sisters wanted you to have this. They said you did their work and that you'd understand."

I carefully unwrapped the gift and saw it was a newly carved soapstone plaque, very similar in color and texture to the one they had given me at the convent, although not in shape. This one was an inverted triangle, slightly rounded at the corners, no sharp edges, smooth to the touch. On its surface was a holy cross with a dove embossed upon it, wings spread parallel to the crossbar, its body perfectly perpendicular, sky to ground. Most importantly, the dove was flying *down* the cross, a sense of purpose in its flight. No hesitation. Total confidence. Absolute faith.

Irene smiled and said, "The sisters felt it was the perfect gift for you."

20

Silence is consent and all it takes for evil to prevail is for one good woman to do nothing.

—from *Crossing to Avalon*
by Jean Shinoda Bolen, M.D.

Eight months after Sister Gloria's death, the day before Halloween, I hit the play button on the office answering machine. It had been two years, but I instantly recognized the voice on the recording.

"I don't know if you remember us, but I thought you should know that Marissa has been asking for you. She's never really stopped, but recently she's been asking more frequently."

Ann Marie didn't make it sound urgent, but I immediately dialed her number. No one was home, so I left a message on their answering machine for Marissa, choosing my words carefully, not knowing what the situation was or who might be listening. "Hi, Marissa, it's Roseanne. Of course I remember you.

I love you. How are you doing, sweetheart? Here's my number, call me anytime."

I was out of the office part of the day but when I returned there was another message. I could hear Ann Marie in the background telling Marissa to say "Hi" to Roseanne. Marissa giggled a "Hi" and then said, "I miss you and want to come see you." Ann Marie came on the line and said she'd like to make an appointment. This time when I called back they were home.

"Thank you for leaving the message for Marissa," Ann Marie said. "The sound of your voice actually calmed her down. She's been crying wildly and uncontrollably, not sleeping, everything just like before. It's been going on for months now."

Apparently Marissa's demeanor changed so much upon hearing my voice that Ann Marie's mother noticed the difference and wanted to know who Roseanne was. All Ann Marie would tell her was that I was a good friend of Marissa's.

"She must be," her mother replied.

I asked Ann Marie when they could come and she gave the response I had wanted to hear two years earlier.

"Any time."

21

With the first crunch of gravel in the driveway, I was up and on my way to the parking lot. Marissa ran into my arms and we held each other and spun around. "I love you, I love you," I kept saying. And she kept repeating, "I love you, too. I love you, too."

Although she was thin and had dark circles under her eyes, it all seemed to lift away as we held each other in the early morning air. Clearly there was still something missing from her life and I was determined to get to the heart of exactly what it was.

"Marissa, you remember Bear, don't you?" I asked after we were settled in the office.

She said, "Yes."

"Why don't you say hi to him."

I handed Bear to her and he began to slip from her grasp. Not wanting him to hit the floor, she reached for his scarf and it tightened around his neck. I started making choking noises and she began to laugh uncontrollably. Our timing still impeccable, things picked up where they'd left off two years before. Marissa punched, slammed, twisted, and kicked Bear. It was a near-perfect replay of her first visit, with Marissa constantly looking to her mother for instructions and me continually assuring Ann Marie it was all right. The only difference was, we didn't throw Bear back and forth this time. She pretty much beat him up all on her own.

"Has Bear had enough yet?" I asked.

"No."

"Do you want to keep hitting him?"

"Yes," she said and worked him over some more.

After a good, long bout she finally fell to the floor and proclaimed, "I'm tired!"

A few minutes later she was in my lap. "I think you need to talk to Bear," I said.

"That's silly."

"You need to tell him you're having nightmares and ask him to help you with them."

"No," she said, pointing out, "bears don't talk."

"Well, my bear does. He talks and he's a good listener too. Really, go ahead and give him a try."

She might throw, hit, and kick him, but there was no way she was going to talk to a stuffed bear. Finally I said, "Okay, you don't have to talk to him, but if you listen carefully, get very quiet inside, and put his mouth to your ear, I think he might talk to you."

She held him to her ear and didn't say anything, but her eyes grew wide, waiting for something to happen.

"What is he saying?" I asked.

"Bears don't talk," she repeated, waiting for my reaction.

"Oh, I don't know. I think if you get very quiet and still . . ." I said, using my voice hypnotically, " . . . really, really quiet, then you can hear him. Shssssh. Listen. Be very still, very quiet. Still and quiet. Listen now. Shssssh. Listen."

Her head began to nod slightly.

"It's okay, close your eyes and listen, shhhhh, listen."

Her eyes kept fluttering open.

"It's all right, it's all right. Shssssh."

I could feel her body relax and melt into mine.

"Bear wants to tell you something."

Without thinking about it, she pulled his face to hers, this time really wanting to hear. When the moment seemed right, I whispered in Bear's voice, "*Give me your nightmares, Marissa. I know what to do with them.*"

She didn't say anything or respond in any way.

"Give me all of your nightmares. Every single one."

Her eyes remained closed and after a moment, I spoke in my normal voice, "Are you done? Did you give Bear all your nightmares?

"Yes."

"Are you sure?"

"I think so."

"Oh. I don't know. I think you should put Bear back to your ear and see if he has anything else to say."

She held him without hesitation and I mouthed over her shoulder to Ann Marie, "Did anything happen recently to set this off?"

Ann Marie nodded and said she'd tell me after the session. I already had a pretty good idea what it might have been. The trauma was all too evident: Marissa's first chakra was like a withered flower, dark and tipped over to the right; her second was wobbly like a spinning top about to fall; and her third was clogged. She was once again shrouded in the dark mist I had cleared away two years before.

As Bear whispered to Marissa, I kept trying to get my hand onto the front of her belly and she kept pushing it away. It was disturbingly reminiscent of my experience with Margaret, although the differences between them far outweighed the similarities—for Margaret, the intrusion was very precise, while for Marissa, it was systemic.

"You've been having tummy aches, haven't you, Marissa?"

"Yes," Marissa said.

"It's okay," I said. "Close your eyes. Just close your eyes."

"Give me your nightmares," Bear told her again. "All of them. Give me your nightmares. Every single one."

I held her in silence as I finished clearing, balancing, and repairing her chakras, opening my eyes sometime after she opened hers. We had made significant progress but the healing involved more than the distortions in her field. Marissa desperately needed a level of protection she was not currently receiving; she was not nearly old enough to have developed the defenses needed to withstand whatever was triggering her hysteria.

I followed Marissa's eyes to the tabletop next to us and there, all by itself, was a small red, wooden heart—a gift from a student. I picked it up and gave it to her.

"This is Bear's heart," I said. "He wants you to have it. He needs you to keep it so you'll never forget how much he loves you."

She held it in her hands a moment, all excited, and then stopped and turned to her mother.

"Is it okay, Mom? Can I have it?"

"If it's okay with Roseanne."

"It's not up to me, it's up to Bear. After all, it's his heart. See what he has to say."

She immediately picked up Bear and held him to her.

Voice cracking a bit, Bear whispered, *"This is a symbol of my love so you remember you're in my heart forever."*

She appeared quite pleased and, after inspecting the heart thoroughly, made a little fist around it as if to proclaim ownership.

This was the appointment they hadn't kept two years ago and now we had come full circle. There was a good chance this would be the last time I'd see Marissa and I so much wanted to give her something more—anything, everything. They hadn't brought a camera and I didn't have one so there was no way to have our picture taken together as she once requested. I looked around the room; surely there was something here for her, something more than a little wooden heart.

"Marissa, do you by any chance like flowers?"

She said, "Oh yes, very much," and described her bedroom which was wallpapered with flowers—sunflowers, her favorite kind.

"I'm not surprised. I wonder if you'd like to add one to your collection?" Pointing to the stained-glass flower that was hanging in the window, I asked, "How would you like that flower for your bedroom window?"

She got all excited and gasped, "Yes, yes, yes!"

I thought it was probably a silly gift to give a child, but her excitement appeared genuine. I handed the glass flower to her and told her to be careful with it. She again looked to her mother for permission.

"Mom, can I have it?"

"It's up to Roseanne."

"Can I really have it?" she asked me.

"Well, I'm a little jealous that Bear got to give you a present and I didn't. So, as a favor to me, I think you should accept my gift too."

It wasn't a fresh cut flower, but it was a flower all the same and just fine with Marissa. She stood there looking utterly adorable with the heart in one hand and the flower in the other. But although her system now appeared healthy and sta-ble, I still had the nagging sense that whatever had been miss-ing from her life was still not there.

Ann Marie started getting Marissa ready to leave and I watched with the knowledge that the healing was incomplete, some element was not in place, and the probability of a relapse was still present. They were halfway through the office door when I looked over at the couch and blurted out, "Marissa, wait!" They stopped, and I heard myself softly say, "I think you're forgetting something."

She turned, a quizzical look on her face.

"I hear Bear calling you," I said.

Her large eyes grew larger. "What does he want?" she said, looking to me for the answer.

"I don't know, I think you should go ask him."

She rushed to the couch, snatched up Bear, and shook him a little as if to wake him up.

"What is it, Bear?" she said. "Please, Bear, tell me what's the matter?" Shaking him a little harder, she continued, "Bear, Bear. What do you want? Please talk to me."

"Better hold him to your ear and close your eyes so you can hear what he's saying," I said.

She sat on the couch and closed her eyes. *"Take me with you,"* Bear gently told her. *"I've fallen in love with you and I'll miss you terribly if you leave without me. I want to go home with you. Please don't leave without me."*

"Oooh," Marissa sighed.

"It looks like Bear wants to go home with you," I said. "I think you'd better take him."

She stood up, absolutely still for a second, and then yelped, "Wow! Could I? Could I?"

"It's not up to me. If he wants to go home with you, that's his decision."

She rocked him in her arms and cradled his head.

"He's yours now and you have to take very good care of

146

him. You must listen to him when he has something to tell you and entrust him with all your bad dreams."

She hugged me again and again in the parking lot until I finally put her down and she happily climbed in the car. Marissa spoke up as Ann Marie helped her with the seat belt, "I'm going to put Bear between Mom and I so he'll be safe."

She was thoroughly involved with Bear and kept changing his position on the seat, from side to lap to side, trying to figure out how best to take care of him. Ann Marie seemed on the verge of saying something, her eyes moist, the weight of the world no longer on her shoulders. By the time we arrived at the other side of the car, the tears were running down her cheeks. "I never took the time to thank you," she said. "The only other person who knows what you've done for us is Teresa."

"That's okay. You're more than welcome, Ann Marie."

"I know you're wondering what caused Marissa's relapse and I'm afraid it's our fault. Despite our efforts, she saw her uncle in May. That's when the nightmares returned."

Although we had never discussed the subject in great detail, I had been extremely clear about this two years before. "I thought it was understood he was never to get near her again."

"I know, but it wasn't intentional. We went to a family event and didn't know he was going to be there. We tried our best to keep Marissa from seeing him, but it just didn't work out that way."

I interrupted her and put my hands on both her shoulders. "Ann Marie, this man cannot be near your daughter until she is old enough to defend herself and even then, I'd question your parenting if you let him get anywhere near her. It is up to *you* to make sure she does not see him until she is able to protect herself. Please believe me. This is vital to Marissa's well-being."

The final piece of the puzzle fell into place: Ann Marie's struggle with her own sense of well-being and personal strength, the timidness I'd sensed upon first meeting her, the frightened part that didn't feel free to talk openly on the phone. She simply didn't have the support she needed to stand up on her child's behalf; she had to do it alone without the aid of her husband or her mother. The strength that comes from support was the link; that is what Marissa needed, that was what was missing. My final task was to come out and directly tell Ann Marie, very specifically, exactly what her job was. *You must not let this man near your child. You must intercede where your daughter cannot. You, Ann Marie, must be present for your daughter's sake and for your own. No matter what. No excuses. Period.*

And if I thought for one second that Ann Marie could not or would not protect her daughter, I would not have hesitated to intercede.

"Do you think she'll continue to have relapses?" she asked.

"If she continues to be exposed to this man she surely will, but if you keep her away from him I think it will be all right. Marissa was molested when she was very, very young, and you have to keep this in mind as she grows up. Should she ever exhibit any behavior that upsets or disturbs you, don't waste a second in getting her to see someone. And I'd be happy to be that someone. So stay in touch and let me know how she's doing, even if it's just once every few years. You have a place you can call. For always. Forever."

Ann Marie instigated the hug this time and I could feel the strength of her resolve. We said our good-byes and she entered the car to discover the seating arrangement had been rethought. Marissa proudly announced that Bear couldn't possibly sit up front and had taken him into the back seat with her where he'd have a seat belt of his own. She made it clear that it was her responsibility to make sure he was safe.

"Good-bye, Marissa. And good luck. Call me if you need me."

Only after they were gone did it occur to me that there was a powerful symbolism to the simple gifts I gave her that day: the wooden heart, a symbol of love that endures; the flower, a metaphor for growth, the courage, and will to live with the intention to move toward the light; and Bear, the wisdom of unreason—talking to a stuffed bear is not necessarily rational, but if that bear can hold nightmares, it is a wise choice. Of course, metaphors are just metaphors, and beyond this symbolic trinity of wisdom, courage, and love lay its embodiment, found every day in a mother's embrace.

I returned to my office only to be confronted by the empty space on my couch, and in that emptiness I could see my own reflection, which I hadn't seen since I was very young. . . .

Once upon a time, a little girl stood in front of a huge old mirror and danced and sang and loved what she saw. Everyday she would spend hours and hours making funny faces, posing and laughing, staring at her own image, totally impressed, in awe, in love. She thought she was talented and exquisitely beautiful, desirable, irresistible in fact, and just about the most marvelous creature on the face of the Earth. Never for a moment, not for one single second, did it ever occur to her that this behavior was unacceptable. For her, looking in the mirror had nothing to do with vanity and everything to do with absolute, pure pleasure.

The little girl usually walked home from elementary school, skipping and hopping, her feet barely touching the ground. Sometimes she'd pretend to be blind or lame, mimicking classmates she saw that day, wondering what it was like to walk in their shoes, never missing an opportunity to catch her reflection in every window she passed. Sometimes she'd lift her skirt to adjust her slip, secure in the knowledge that if she kept her eyes closed no one else could see.

One particular day, she and her friend Prudence were walking home from school together when a car pulled up next to them. A man they did not recognize rolled down the driver's window and said he needed directions. Eager to be helpful, and being more outgoing than Prudence, the little girl spoke up.

"You're facing the wrong way," she said. "Go to the end of the street, turn around, and go down the other way."

He drove off and the two girls watched as he turned around and started passing them on the way back. To their surprise, he stopped again and this time leaned over and rolled down the passenger window.

"Sorry, I forgot the directions. Could you give them to me again?"

The little girl told him again and, after he drove away, she and Prudence turned off the main road and onto a side street. This time when the man pulled up next to them, the little girl had the growing sense that something was wrong.

"I'm really sorry," he said, "but I'm a bit hard of hearing. Could you come a little closer and give me those directions just one more time?"

The little girl, frightened but wanting to help, said "sure" and started to approach the car. Prudence broke into a run when the man opened the door and grabbed her friend. As he began to drive away, the little girl thought it odd that he was wearing a shirt and nothing else. And while her mind made up its own explanation of what he was doing with his other hand, she knew it was not good, and it added to her terror.

As the car picked up momentum, she struggled against the man's grasp, too stunned to scream. He nearly had her all the way inside when the car started to head uphill and the door suddenly slammed into his forearm. The impact loosened his grip just enough so that she could roll away. She didn't know what he did next because she took off running and didn't stop until she was home, in bed and under the covers.

Up in her room, she knew one thing for sure: she was bad; something really bad had just happened and there was no way she was going to tell anybody about it, ever. The events of that afternoon would eventually fade and be all but forgotten, and the days of innocence long gone before the little girl even realized that she no longer enjoyed dancing and singing and posing in front of the mirror; she no longer enjoyed seeing her own reflection. When exactly it happened she did not know, but she had stopped believing. . . .

The evening after the attempted kidnapping, that day long ago with Prudence, I was interviewed by the police in my living room. I sat on one couch and they on the other. "What kind of car was it? What was he wearing? What did he do to you?"

I answered all of their questions as best I could. "It was a station wagon. It was white. He was wearing a plaid shirt and nothing else. Nothing happened, nothing bad." As soon as the interrogation was over, I asked, "May I please be excused?"

"Is there anything else you'd like to tell us?"

"No."

"Are you sure you're okay?"

"Yes, I'm sure."

I quietly left the room, went upstairs to my bedroom, and closed the door. I didn't begin to cry until I was alone and certain no one could hear.

It would be more than twenty years before I'd learn one of the most significant details surrounding this event. The day after the attempted kidnapping, my mom and dad organized all the shop owners, all the parents, and all the people who owned houses along the route the children walked. They set up an elaborate telephone network and, when school let out, they'd stand outside of their stores and homes, making sure all was as it should be. I didn't notice and never suspected that every day as I made my way home, I was being watched over and protected—along with all the other children.

I didn't need Bear any more. I knew I was cared for and watched over. Bear had been given to me years ago while I was still working for the financial institution, a Christmas present from a thoughtful friend who was also single and living the solitary life. One busy, forgettable afternoon, I discovered him at my desk, sitting in my chair. The note pinned to him read: "So you always have someone to talk to." He'd been fine company all these years, always present and available, a great listener. I'd miss him a great deal, but he was where he belonged. It was time for both of us to move on. Today a mother and baby monkey occupy that same spot on my couch and where once a protecting bear stood guard against loneliness, a mother and child now reside in peace.

PART THREE

Faith

Amanda

22

Playmate, come out and play with me
And bring your dollies three
Climb up the apple tree
Slide down my rainbow
Into my cellar door
And we ll be jolly friends for ever more

Ruth and John lived in a quiet bedroom community of modest two-story colonials and both worked in the medical field. They spent the first ten years of their marriage unable to conceive, so it came as something of a shock when Ruth discovered she was pregnant. The birth of Amanda was like a fresh start for the couple and seemed to soften something they hadn't realized had hardened. Their baby was tender and easy to be around. She only cried when she was hurt. No temper tantrums. Loved people. A gentle disposition. Ruth often said her daughter was every parent's dream.

The couple worked a staggered schedule so one of them would always be home to care for Amanda. Ruth came home early one night and, when John wasn't downstairs in front of the television as usual, she assumed the baby had wakened and he was trying to get her back to sleep. She tiptoed up the stairs and found him standing over the crib, crying, Amanda sound asleep.

"What are you doing?"

"I just had to look at her again."

"But why are you crying?"

"Because she's so perfect."

Amanda grew and was in every way a normal child: getting muddy in the back yard, playing patty-cake with her girl friends, always excited to get a new toy. Yet there was something in the things she occasionally said, and a faraway look in her eyes, that seemed to transcend childhood. But these moments were brief and, before you knew it, she would be typical again.

Being fond of pretty things, from an early age Amanda took an active interest in what she wore. She would stand in front of the big mirror in her parent's room and Ruth would help her select a ribbon to match the dress she had picked out. Amanda even chose the wallpaper in her bedroom. It had little hearts and tiny blue flowers on a white background.

The first indications that all was not well were whispered so softly they could serve no other purpose than to later return in the guise of a self-assault for not having acted on them sooner. Despite any later doubts, Ruth was keenly alert to the early manifestations. When she'd lay Amanda down to change her diaper, the baby sometimes appeared disoriented and would extend her tiny arms outward, tightly grabbing hold of the bed. She also noticed that Amanda fell from time to time and, while this in itself did not seem out of the ordinary, Amanda's reaction to falling struck Ruth as somewhat unusual. Whereas other children would put their hands out when they lost their balance, Amanda seemed to lack this reflex and would take her falls full force, often face first. It was common for her to have bruises on her forehead, particularly around her hairline. As the weeks and months went by, other slight anomalies appeared in Amanda's behavior and it seemed to Ruth they were, in some way, connected to her daughter's sense of balance. Still, it was all fairly subtle.

Hoping to be reassured, Ruth brought Amanda to a series of pediatricians; via her connections, she knew who the top practitioners were and sought them out. The doctors performed all the basic neurological tests and dismissed her concerns as those of an overprotective, first-time mother. The medical advice she received ranged from "don't tie your daughter's shoes so tight" to "don't buy sneakers with a heavy tread." But it wasn't motherly instinct that was motivating Ruth, it was a sense she developed while working with patients in the hospital—and she was anything but reassured.

After a great deal of prodding from Ruth, one doctor finally ordered deeper neurological tests. Ruth knew he did it just to shut her up. The tests proved inconclusive and he referred the case to a pediatric neurologist. In the neurologist's preliminary exam, he found nothing wrong but, toward the end of the visit, wrote a note and pushed it across the desk to Ruth. It read, "What do you see?" She wrote a reply and slid it back to him, "Just pick her up, hold her as you would any other child, and then lean her backwards a little bit."

When he tried this, Amanda grabbed his tie and desperately held on. It was enough to convince him to order an MRI. He did not consider the situation to be particularly critical, and the MRI was scheduled for six weeks from that day.

The following weekend, Amanda began displaying symptoms of what is frequently referred to as waking nausea. She would throw up once or twice in the morning and then be fine the rest of the day. Ruth knew this was sometimes the result of excessive cranial pressure. The fluid builds up during sleep, while a person is in a horizontal position and then, when she sits up or stands, some of this fluid drains out of the head and into the stomach, causing nausea. Hoping this wasn't the case, Ruth reported these symptoms to the neurologist. He had her stay on the line and set up a conference call with the medical center. "I want them to hear what you're saying," he said.

Within two hours, Amanda was in the MRI. When it was over, Ruth and John were told there was a tumor near the center of their daughter's brain. Amanda was immediately admitted to the medical center and, forty-eight hours later, underwent surgery. The biopsy confirmed that the tumor was malignant and inoperable. She was two years old.

Amanda continued to grow and the tumor attempted to grow; it was held in check by a regimen of intravenous chemotherapy. She had to stay in the hospital during treatment periods, which were scheduled every three weeks, and the chemotherapy irritated her bladder to the point where she no longer had the control she had recently gained. But although she had to wear a diaper again, Amanda was uncomplaining and quickly became a favorite of both the staff and patients.

Despite her own discomfort, Amanda was deeply concerned about the other children in the ward and insisted upon meeting them. Ruth would help her daughter push the pole that held the chemo-drip down the hall and Amanda would totter into a room, over to a child's bed, and say, "Hi, my name is Amanda. This is my mommy, Ruth. I have three cats, one dog, and a boo-boo in my head." And, in this manner, Ruth, John, and Amanda tried to sneak past the years.

When she was five years old, the family took a trip to New York City. Amanda couldn't have been more excited and talked of nothing else in the days leading up to their departure. Nor was she disappointed when they arrived in Manhattan; there was plenty to see and Amanda had more than enough energy for the task. She was not, in any sense, overwhelmed by the huge crowds that lined Fifth Avenue and greeted several passersby, many of whom responded warmly.

Outside the Metropolitan Museum of Art, she spotted an old man on a bench smoking a cigarette and, before Ruth and

John could stop her, she sat down next to him. "I bet you know that smoking can hurt you," she said, putting her hand on the man's knee and patting it. "Sometimes when things hurt your body, you wind up in the hospital. You know, everybody that goes to the hospital doesn't always get to come home. Somebody loves you, and that would make them cry."

Ruth and John apologized to the man and led Amanda into the museum. She was quite taken by what she saw inside and asked a million questions about every exhibit. They were easier to answer than some of the other questions she'd been asking recently, like the ones about what happens to people after they die. They were easier to answer than the ones Ruth and John had asked that morning in the office of the renowned pediatric neurosurgeon, whom they had come to New York to see.

But nobody had any answers.

23

I certainly didn't have any answers—plenty of wonderful questions, though, and I'd soon have more: like how did I get myself into this and how will any of us survive it? My practice, at the time, so many years ago now, consisted exclusively of adult patients. Amanda was the first child I saw professionally, and she was much more than that. She was the question and the answer.

It was a full three months before Thanksgiving. I didn't know at the time that this would be the last year I visited the homeless shelter; I didn't know my experience with Amanda would forever change my understanding of charity and inspire what would become my annual holiday prayer. Amanda was the reason for all the calls and it was she who brought me Margaret, Marissa, Alex, and even Sister Gloria.

It was six-thirty by the time my last appointment left and I was more than ready to leave the office when the phone rang. I thought about not answering it; calls can be long, involved, and inescapable when you're a therapist, and I just wanted to go home.

"Hello," I said, trying to sound alive.

"Hello. Is this Roseanne?" It was a woman's voice.

"Yes."

"I'm so glad I reached you. A friend told me about you after she heard one of your lectures. She suggested I call. I'd like to make an appointment, if that's possible." Her voice sounded calm but I could tell she was rattled inside . . . like a lot of the people who call me.

"Why don't you tell me something about yourself and why you want to see me."

"My name is Ruth, and I thought you might be able to help us. My family and I will only be in town for a few weeks."

"Help you with what?"

"Well," she hesitated, "I'm not calling for myself. It's not about me. It's about my daughter."

"How old is she?"

"She's five."

"And what's the situation?"

"She's been diagnosed with a brain tumor and the doctors have given her only ten weeks to live."

It took me several seconds to respond; I'd never been here before. "I'm so sorry to hear that. What's her name?"

"Amanda."

I repeated her name, searching for something appropriate to say. Finally I said, "Ruth, this must be extremely difficult for you."

She didn't bother to respond to this and continued. "I know you're busy and difficult to get an appointment with, but I'm afraid you're our last hope."

I felt the water rising; it had reached my neck and was tickling my chin. My schedule was full and there was no space for new patients. Certainly no room to be anybody's last hope. "You said you were only in town for a few weeks?"

"Yes, we're staying with relatives in the area. Will you see her?"

"I've got my appointment book right here," I heard myself say as if it were someone else's book, as if I could handle this. "Let's see when I can get you in. What's good for you?"

"Anytime this week. Anytime you can see us."

"All right. Then how's tomorrow morning, early?" It was the only uncommitted time I had.

"Do you need to know more details about the situation? Should I bring her medical records?"

"Bring what you have and we'll talk when I see you."

We made an appointment for the following morning. I gave her directions and she thanked me several times before saying good-bye. I was somewhat surprised she hadn't asked me about my fee as most people do, until the obvious occurred to me: the life of her child had no price. By the time I put the phone down, I was standing on the bottom of the ocean.

24

The sun wasn't high enough to reach the window yet, so the office was full of shadows when I heard the car pull into the driveway. Although their appointment was still half an hour away, I knew it was Ruth and her daughter. I listened as the car doors slammed shut and they made their way across the gravel driveway. Ruth told me on the phone that she and her husband worked as medical professionals, not doctors but skilled technicians, which added to my insecurities about my qualifications. I greeted them at the door and, after they entered, I got my first good look at Amanda.

She looked like a little cherub-faced angel, the kind I sometimes see in stores. She had large blue eyes that played peek-a-boo behind the light brown bangs of her pageboy hair-cut, her skin creamy, her face round and full. There was a slight bluish cast to her lips, in contrast to the crimson glow of her cheeks. She was beautiful, stunningly so.

She entered the office, moving past me with breathtaking serenity, and took a seat on my mother's old couch next to Bear. I turned on the desk lamp so I could see her in a better light, but the shadow that fell across her tiny face remained.

"Amanda," Ruth gently admonished. "Don't you think you should say hello to Roseanne?"

"Hello," Amanda said.

"Hi, Amanda. You can play with Bear, if you like, while I talk to your mommy. Go ahead, put him on your lap. I can tell he already likes you. He sometimes gets a little warm with his wool hat and scarf on, so you can take them off if he wants you to."

Ruth appeared much the way she sounded on the phone: salt of the earth, Americana, a softly rounded woman of medium height with the same short brown hair as her daughter. She was dressed casually, wearing little or nothing in the way of jewelry or accessories. She was not a fashion plate, but neat and well put together. There was a competence and intelligence about her. She had surely turned over every traditional and nontraditional medical rock in an attempt to find a cure for her daughter. Now they were here, and I prayed that, should I be unable to help the situation, *please don't let me make it worse.*

"Why don't you have a seat over here, Ruth. I need you to fill out a form."

Ruth seemed anxious to please and do everything just

right as if, in some way, her behavior might influence the outcome of her daughter's illness. She sat up straight and she began to meticulously fill out the paperwork.

In another world, a few feet away, Amanda put the teddy bear down and, leaving the couch, ventured farther into the room. Unable to take my eyes from her, I watched as she explored the office, occasionally touching a brightly colored crystal or picking up a miniature statue. She responded readily when Ruth looked up from the questionnaire and told her to put whatever it was down.

"It's all right," I told Ruth. "She can do anything she wants here."

Ruth started to give me the kind of look only a mother can deliver and then thought better of it. She told me about Amanda's medical history with a detached professionalism, that was both impressive and unnerving. Apparently she'd been doing this for quite some time, telling doctors and various health care professionals the story over and over again. As she spoke, I was increasingly aware of how controlled and stoic she was, answering my questions much as a scientist might. The technical terminology didn't mean that much to me, having little training in medicine, but I could see she was doing a hell of a job holding herself together, and I liked her all the more for it. I would have been hysterical in her position.

Despite the interaction with Ruth, I was constantly aware of Amanda and had been from the moment she entered the office. I could feel her presence in the room and, oddly enough, she seemed content, totally at peace, not anxious at all, really quite the normal five-year-old. She was light and graceful and coordinated enough to walk perfectly well. But as I continued to observe her movements, an occasional wobbliness, in a most terrible way, erased any doubts I might have had as to the severity of her condition. I watched her long enough to know that the situation was extremely bleak.

Picking up Bear, I followed her to the wall of diplomas and sat down on the floor behind her. Without a word she turned around and sat on my lap, gently taking him from me. I felt her tiny body press ever so slightly against my chest and I took the opportunity to begin the examination. There was something a little crazy about this whole situation: the mother of a dying child, answering questions and filling out forms in a business-as-usual manner; me, going to pieces inside; and a child with ten weeks to live who seemed, in the deepest sense, perfectly fine.

Ruth got up and handed me the questionnaire. Amanda remained in my lap, quietly singing and gently stroking Bear's fine white fur. For a moment I thought I recognized the melody.

"He loves to be petted," I said. "Can you hear him purr?"

Amanda turned from Bear and looked me square in the face. Quietly, and with the assurance of a saint, she said, "Of course."

Her attention returned to Bear and I began to look over the intake form. My eyes locked on the part that read, "List the details you feel to be pertinent to your case." Ruth had written: "Amanda now has moderate hydrocephilia from a tumor that is blocking the CS fluid. She is scheduled for a shunt in nine days. They tell us she only has weeks to live and I am seeking any help with the quality of her life and any extension possible." Seeing it in black and white, as this little angel stirred in my lap, made it all the more real.

Ruth later explained that a shunt was an operation in which the fluid is drained as a means of reducing the pressure on the brain. In this case, it was part of a short-term medical strategy. If I was shaking as I held her, Amanda gave no indication she was aware of it. I looked up at Ruth and for the first time in our brief acquaintance, there were tears in her eyes.

"There's a box of tissues on the table," I said. "I could use a couple myself." Ruth and I exchanged smiles. "Why don't you make yourself comfortable. Amanda and I are going to play for awhile."

Amanda, still in my lap, seemed oblivious or, perhaps, uninterested in the surrounding drama. I asked her to do to Bear whatever I did to her and she accurately mimicked my actions. She was cooperative and extremely well behaved as we played together. And while some of her extraordinary composure could be attributed to exceedingly poor muscle strength, working with her, I could feel there was more to it than that.

After a few minutes, we got up and I helped her onto the table, hoping to maintain a playful mood, trying to keep her from identifying any of this with her previous medical experiences. Amanda allowed me to examine her with extraordinary grace and maturity, absolutely sure of herself, a pro who had been through all kinds of examinations many times before.

What I found was difficult to reconcile. Although a tumor was invading her brain, ravaging her system, in some more profound sense, there was absolutely nothing wrong. She was perfectly aligned and at peace with her destiny. As I realized this, a rush, a flood of divinity, filled the room. It was accompanied by a golden hued light of extreme clarity and intensity—blinding, although it did not make me squint.

I helped Amanda off the table and she wandered away. She had no need of my services. For her, the decisions were already made, and they were hers to make. I hadn't spoken during most of the session and had no idea what I was going to say to Ruth. To make things worse, when I looked over at her, she was starting to write out a check.

"I'm writing you a check. Just tell me how much to make it out for," Ruth said, making it clear there would be no bickering about amounts.

"That's not necessary, Ruth. I'd prefer if you'd let me give this to you." I had no intention of not charging, but in view of the situation, accepting payment was out of the question.

"Don't be ridiculous. I absolutely insist upon paying you. I appreciate your taking the time to see Amanda."

"I know you want to pay me and I appreciate that. But I

can't accept payment. I don't want to argue about it. I just need it to be this way, okay?"

"Well, all right. But I'm not going to forget about this."

"I know you won't, Ruth."

Ruth began helping Amanda into her coat. She must have sensed what I was thinking because she hesitated ever so slightly before asking, "Should I make another appointment, would it help to bring Amanda back?" It was the question I didn't want her to ask: *Can you save my baby's life?*

I took a deep breath before responding. "Ruth, you look awfully stressed out. I mean, who wouldn't be? I think you're the one who needs to come back." Having no idea what her reaction to this suggestion might be, I pressed the point just the same. It's not like there was a choice. "I'd really like it if you could come back by yourself, if you think you have time before you return to Virginia. Would you like that?"

Unexpectedly, she allowed a small sob to escape and a moment later she came into my arms. She quietly said, "I would love to. I would love to talk to somebody."

I said, "Of course, you would," and for the first time felt that maybe I could be of some help.

She made an appointment for the following day and was to come by herself, without her daughter. I went to bed that night thinking about the things I hadn't told her that afternoon. As I lay awake for many hours, Amanda's image remained fresh in my mind. It was the first time I had seen a condition of this severity in anyone, let alone a child. She had almost no color left in her field, and the little that was still there was beginning to dissolve. There was inevitability in what I saw and no relief from the feelings that accompanied the vision—not even the knowledge that Amanda was securely in the company of angels and had been for some time. There were two of them present during most of the session, one on either side of her. They were beautiful, comforting, powerful. They were the angels of death.

It wasn't until the next morning that I realized something previously beyond my grasp: Ruth had not brought Amanda to me, it was the other way around. Amanda had brought her mother.

25

"Although it's impossible for me to fully understand what you're going through, I can only imagine how horrible it must be." Ruth sat across from me and nodded her head. Now that we were alone, I was determined to help her explore the things I knew she was feeling but wasn't expressing, to help her speak the unspeakable.

"I don't mean to feel sorry for myself, but no mother—nobody—should have to go through this. It's so unfair," she said. "There's no right time or place to express my anger and pain, not even with John. I know everybody wants me to feel better, and I'm grateful for that, but how can I? Nothing's okay, and I don't think it'll ever be okay."

"You're right, and this can't be easy for either you or John. How is he handling this?" I'd been wondering where he was in all this.

"You know how it is. We're both trying to be strong for each other. We underreact to everything which, instead of helping, has basically undermined the intimacy between us. It's like we're both going through this alone."

"Ruth, in a way, you're right. Nothing and no one, not even John, can truly understand your pain, and no one can take it away." I left it there, although part of me wanted to tell her more, give her something substantial to hold onto. "It's all in God's hands" seemed just too trite, too empty, too impersonal. And yet that was all there was to hold on to.

"Another thing that makes this so unfair is that supposedly we weren't able to have children," Ruth continued. "Amanda was conceived after we had seen all the specialists and given up on having a child of our own. In fact, we were so sure I couldn't become pregnant, we adopted a cat."

She stopped and showed me a picture of their cat, which she kept in her wallet. Like Amanda, the cat appeared to be perfectly content and at peace.

"John can't be holding up that well under this strain," I said. "Who could?"

"Oh, inside I know he's a wreck. Maybe worse than me." She paused a moment. "Do you think it would be helpful for the two of us to see you together?"

It was clear she wished he was with her to be a part of this conversation. "Yes, I think that would be a good idea."

"I wish he could understand me better," she went on. "I really could use more support. Actually, I didn't even realize that until we started talking."

"He's going through the same thing you are. He's just handling it in his own way. It's likely he needs you as much as you need him."

I suggested she bring John to the next appointment, and she agreed to try. I felt good about that. If there was anything I could do for this family, even if it was just helping them communicate and support one another, I wanted to do it.

We talked, and occasionally cried, through the hour. She seemed genuinely relieved there was somebody around who wasn't trying to tell her "it was going to be okay," or to "try not to worry," or that "she'd get through this." Acknowledging just how bad it all was and how helpless she felt confirmed her feelings, and I believe she left with a little less anxiety than she had arrived with. I wanted to think so, anyway.

26

They looked like a couple. They were similar in height and girth, and both exuded a healthy heartland solidity. I welcomed them into the office and watched as they sat on the same couch, he on one side and she on the other. I found this somewhat surprising, having the preconceived notion that parents of a dying child would be clinging to each other for dear life, holding hands, crying on each other's shoulder. As it was, they appeared to be miles apart; two separate ships sailing through the same storm.

John was on the round side, with glasses and reddish-brown hair. His beard was relatively close cropped and, like Ruth, he was well manicured in every way. When they first arrived, they both shook my hand in a businesslike manner, reinforcing my sense that kicking and screaming were not a part of this couple's repertoire. He appeared even more restrained than she. I sat down across from them.

"John, you know Ruth and I talked for quite awhile the other day. This must be the most difficult thing you've ever had to endure." I paused, giving John an opening he didn't take. Somewhere in there was a dam ready to burst. "How is all of this affecting you? I mean, how do you manage to hold up under this much emotional stress?"

"It's difficult," he replied without showing any emotion.

Before I could ask my next question, Ruth spoke up, "Come on, John, you feel more than that."

"I said it's difficult," he defended himself before turning back to me. "It's very hard. Of course I find this very hard to handle."

Ruth needed to see that John's emotions were equal to hers, that this was happening to them, not just her. She'd been trying to match her husband's understatement step for step, believing it wasn't acceptable to break down in the face of his restraint.

"What's going on with you, Ruth?" I asked.

"I feel incredibly bad and incredibly angry. I'm angry about what's happening to my daughter and hurt by my husband." She confronted John. "Yes, hurt, by the fact you're not there for me and not giving me the support I need."

"I'm just trying to hold it together for all of us," he quietly replied. "If I just let it go and let out how I really feel, I don't know what might happen."

John needed to be stoic in order to keep functioning. This was how he kept it together. He just put his head down and did his thing, be it driving his daughter to the hospital or going to work. It was business as usual, just one step at a time. Unfortunately, it was tearing their relationship apart just when they needed each other the most. As the session proceeded, the buried emotions began to surface.

"I have to tell you, John, the way you've been handling this, so controlled, makes me feel like you don't really care." Ruth's hands were clenched together, knuckles white from the pressure. I could feel the tension building as her eyes filled with tears. Judging by John's reaction, I'd seen more of her tears than he had.

He responded with some emotional depth of his own. "What do you expect me to do? What do you want from me?"

"To see that it hurts you as much as it hurts me."

"Don't you understand, this is killing me. I don't know how else to act or what else to do. I want to protect you and Amanda, but I can't. I'm sorry, but I can't shield you from this and I don't know how to make it better. No matter what I say, no matter what I do, we're losing her, Ruth. How do you think I feel? My daughter is dying and I can't save her." His helplessness took all the air out of the room and for one long moment we sat there frozen.

And then they were in each other's arms, quiet tears sliding slowly down their cheeks.

I saw Ruth one last time before the family returned to Virginia. She came by herself, again early, before the first scheduled patient of the day. We talked mostly about her and not Amanda, but she still seemed to hold a great deal inside. I hadn't done anything particularly special or effective for her and, as we hugged good-bye, I felt my own version of helplessness.

I told her she could call any time and to keep me informed.

As she drove away, I felt grateful for what remained unsaid. In spite of any indications to the contrary, and although she never even came close to saying it, Ruth was still hoping against hope that someone could save the life of her only child.

27

About ten days after our last meeting, Ruth called.

"Well, I just wanted to call and let you know how things were going."

"I'm glad you did. What's happening?"

"We took Amanda to the hospital today. There was no change in her condition, so they went ahead with the shunt. She's okay; the surgery went all right. It will help her for awhile."

"Are you okay?"

"Yes, I think so. I just thought it might be helpful for you to know what was going on."

"Of course. You did the right thing. I want to know everything that's going on with Amanda," then quickly added, "but I'm just as interested in what's happening with you."

"Well, I know how busy you are. . . ."

"It's okay. Really. You can talk to me about anything that comes up. In fact, I'd appreciate it if you did."

"Thanks. I'll call you after we know a little more."

"How's John?"

"He's still working full-time. It's the only way he can deal with his pain. You know, he's so good with Amanda. He loves her so."

"I know he does, and he loves you too. How are the two of you doing?"

"John's trying, he really is. It's still difficult, but we're talking and touching a little more. And I'm trying to be better at understanding him and the way he's dealing with this."

"A lot of couples have great difficulty getting through this kind of crisis. Many don't make it."

"Boy, I can believe that."

"That's why I'm so impressed with the two of you. You're both still there for each other."

"We're trying, but we're running out of strength."

"As anybody would. I know it's not much but, for what it's worth, you and John are constantly in my prayers and so is Amanda."

"Thank you." I could hear her take a deep breath. "Well, I guess I'd better get back at it."

"Promise me you'll stay in touch."

"I promise."

"Then I'll talk to you soon."

I hung up, knowing there would be more calls.

The next time I heard from Ruth was on the first day of autumn—or possibly, the first day it felt like autumn. I was rooting for a solitary maple leaf the wind was nudging across the empty parking lot when she called to tell me about a discussion she had had with Amanda's doctor. Her matter-of-fact timber and medical phraseology in no way masked the portrait of a situation steadily going downhill. Among other things, the doctors told her Amanda would soon lose motor control of her legs which, shortly thereafter, would be followed by an inability to eat.

Ruth and John were wrestling with options of how they might deal with these foretold events, and I could offer no advice. I talked with John briefly and, in his understated style, he readily acknowledged his pain, which seemed no small feat. But this new information about Amanda was having a profound effect on both of them and intensified my concerns for their well-being.

Autumn was definitely here, the first hard frost due any day, and Amanda's condition was continuing to deteriorate. The phone calls from Ruth were updates on her daughter's condition, "progress reports" not being an appropriate description. As Amanda's health went from bad to worse, Ruth and John's despair grew in direct proportion, with more and more panic creeping into Ruth's voice each time we spoke. She was still hoping against hope that Amanda could be saved, and I was still unable or unwilling to say anything that might take away that last hope.

Ruth said she and John decided to care for Amanda at home. It was not a difficult decision for them; being in the field, they had access to state-of-the-art medical equipment.

"That sounds like a lot to take on." Somewhere along the line, I had become the master of enunciating the obvious.

She politely agreed and confided that caring for Amanda was becoming increasingly difficult but that they would have it no other way.

The next phone call came about a week or so later. Ruth left a message on the office machine and although she was trying to sound pragmatic, she was obviously upset. It was evening before I could get back to her.

"Amanda's walking like a drunken sailor," she said, her voice shaking.

"What? What do you mean?"

"She can hardly walk anymore. It's like she's drunk. It just started happening today."

It was easy to picture the progression of Amanda's deterioration from that slight wobble I saw in my office to the events of the day. This time, rather than state the obvious, I mostly listened.

As Amanda's physical condition worsened, Ruth and John had to have additional equipment brought to their house. It also became necessary to hire a full-time nurse, which they did without hesitation.

And the phone calls kept coming.

28

"Ruth?"

"Yeah, it's me."

"Are you all right?"

"Well, I'm not sure." Her voice shook. "Can you talk?"

"Of course. What's going on?"

"Something's happening and I don't know what to do about it."

"Tell me. Maybe we can figure it out together."

"I don't know why this has me so upset, but Amanda has started insisting Santa Claus is coming."

"I'm not sure I understand, Ruth."

"She thinks it's Christmas. We keep telling her the costumes and decorations are for Halloween, not Christmas, but she just doesn't seem to get it."

I think she mistook the meaning of my silence because she reminded me that the next day was Halloween. "No matter how many times John or I tell her, she keeps insisting Santa is coming and that it's Christmas. There's just no getting through to her."

"I know this is incredibly difficult for you." God knows. "But, Ruth, I think you should listen to Amanda, she's trying to tell you something."

"What's she trying to tell me?"

"Ruth," I whispered, "Christmas has always meant so much to your family. I think you should listen to Amanda." There was a long, long silence.

"I don't understand what you're saying. I need to know what I should do," she responded, starting to lose what little composure she had left. "What am I supposed to do?"

"Amanda's speaking to you from her heart, not her mind. Listen to her; she knows what she's talking about. Listen to Amanda, Ruth. Santa Claus *is* coming tonight. He's coming so you can have one final Christmas together, so everyone has a chance to say good-bye."

There was more silence and finally a gasp. Through her sobs, Ruth said, "I understand. I know what to do."

That evening, Ruth and John called all their relatives and all of Amanda's friends. They explained that Amanda believed the next day was Christmas and, since it would likely be her last, they'd appreciate it if everyone went along with this. No one refused. That night, Amanda went to bed secure in the knowledge Santa had already taken flight and the next morning would bring a day of her favorite foods, family, and gifts. When they were sure she was asleep, Ruth and John began the daunting task of decorating the house. Come morning, there was no doubt as to what day it was.

The friends and relatives arrived early and placed their gifts, each one wrapped in cheerful Christmas paper, under the brightly lit tree. When everything was in place, they woke

Amanda and brought her downstairs, where the holiday was in full swing. She was delighted, although not surprised, to find the house full of people she loved. Santa had come just as she said he would. With a little bit of help, she opened every one of her presents, kissing and thanking its giver, wondering why so many of them had tears in their eyes. It was the most Christmas-like Christmas any of them had ever known.

The next day, Amanda fell into a complete and irreversible coma. Ruth called that night and said Amanda had been given only a few days to live, two weeks at best. "Although she's in a coma," she told me, "we're going to continue to take care of her here at home."

The doctors told Ruth and John that Amanda would never regain consciousness and would die in her sleep sometime within the given time frame. The couple decided to make sure one of them was with her twenty-four hours a day, talking to her, reading to her, praying for her. John reluctantly kept going to work while Ruth took a leave of absence and remained at home full-time.

Nine days into the coma, Ruth called. "Amanda is still hanging in there," she said, "and I keep talking to her. Do you think she hears me? Do you think she knows I'm there?"

"Of course she knows. She experiences everything you say, think, and feel." I was holding back and Ruth sensed it.

"Is there something else, Roseanne?"

"Ruth, Amanda does know you're there, you and John, and she's not going to let go until the two of you are ready, until she's certain you and John will be okay."

"I don't know what you mean."

"Letting Amanda go, Ruth, is not the same as letting go of loving her."

"I'm not ready for her to die, if that's what you mean," she said firmly. "It's not time and I'm not ready. I'm not ready to let her go!"

"Then don't," I said, as something inside me let go. "Go to

her. Go to her right now and hold her. Hold her tight. Hold Amanda like a mother holds her only child. Hold her in love and total acceptance. Hold her the way you've always wanted to be held, the way God holds us, the way you wish your mother was holding you right now." *The way I wished my mother was holding me.*

A few days later, the phone rang and I knew who it was before I answered. Ruth was devastated, completely exhausted, and deep in pain.

"She's suffering. My baby's suffering." Ruth's training made it impossible for her to ignore what was happening physiologically to Amanda. "She's starving to death; that's what happens at this stage. Oh God, I don't want her to starve. I've seen it before and I don't want my angel to suffer that kind of slow death, Roseanne."

Ruth was certain her daughter was experiencing the pains of a death by starvation and I, a woman who had no children of my own, was supposed to tell her what to do. All I could think was why on Earth am I here and part of this moment, so deeply inside this woman's heartache? I knew Amanda's little body was deteriorating, yet, as I noted when I saw her in my office, she had been coming and going into and out of the physical for quite some time and was well practiced. As with Sister Gloria, dying slowly and not from sudden trauma afforded her this opportunity; it also benefited Ruth and John by providing them time to prepare. It was a blessing with little human comfort.

"Amanda doesn't want to leave until you tell her it's okay for her to go." The plain truth was all there was. There was nothing else.

"I can't do that. I'm not ready to let her go."

"She's hanging on for you and John, Ruth. She's waiting for the two of you to be all right with this. I know this doesn't make sense, but Amanda's fine. She really is and has been all along."

"I want to believe that," she responded, "but I can't tell my daughter it's okay to die. It's not supposed to happen like this. A mother isn't supposed to bury her children. It's not okay and it'll never be okay." Her voice broke and she wasn't able to go on.

"Amanda's in good hands, Ruth. She's made her decision and is at peace with it. The angels are with her."

"I don't want to lose her."

"Of course you don't. And I understand it's not all right this second but you'll know when the moment is at hand. And when it's here, all you need to do is tell Amanda you'll love her forever and that it's all right for her to leave."

"That time will never come. It will never be all right."

"When the time comes, you'll know it, Ruth. You'll know what to do, and you'll know what to say. I know you will."

29

Several days later, Ruth called and told me the rest of the story. She was lying in bed holding Amanda, now shrunken and withered, in her arms. John was asleep in a chair at their side. She would later confide that it happened without any thought on her part; the words just came. Holding Amanda's pale little face in her hands, she said to the only daughter she would ever have, "Its okay for you to go now, sweetie. I'll always love you, and I'll always be your mommy. But it's okay to go. I understand. I really do."

Ruth looked over at John and saw he was awake, listening, in tears. He got up and laid down on the bed so he could put his arms around his wife and daughter.

"Mommy's right," he said. "We'll always love you, but you

don't have to stay here like this any longer for us. We'll miss you so much but, somehow, we'll be okay."

"So you see, it's all right for you to go, Amanda," Ruth joined in. "Your daddy and I will always love you, no matter what. Always."

Upon hearing Ruth and John's words, Amanda—deep in an irreversible coma, a child that was never to wake—opened her eyes, sat up in bed, and said, "Mommy, I'm sorry." Seconds later, she died in Ruth's arms.

It was the bittersweet lesson I first tasted the morning this little girl walked into my office and I knew, beyond any doubt, she was not going to survive. Amanda was prepared to die from the moment I saw her, except she did not want to leave her parents in such a terrible and seemingly hopeless situation. She did not want to leave them until they understood, until she knew they could live and love without her.

Amanda made her choice long before I entered the picture, but what was I to say to Ruth and John? What solace would there have been in telling them that Amanda's life was serving a purpose, that at only five years old and dying from a brain tumor, she was bringing to the world an awareness of how to love and how to let go? How could any explanation, any rationale, bring comfort to parents who were losing their only child?

Amanda didn't need explanations; she was completely accepting of her impending death. She was the first child I'd seen of whom I was one hundred percent certain that her physical body was not going to survive—and it was not a bad thing, not something that needed to be cured or healed. Emanating from this tiny being was a decision made from a greater consciousness, a greater courage, a greater love.

30

It was a raw winter that year, the kind that holds one captive. I spent much of it in quietude, teaching and working with patients, and spoke with Ruth only once during this period.

Spring finally came and found me home preparing for another lecture, which I seemed to be doing increasingly. Ruth called to tell me she and John were returning to the area and wanted to know if I had time to see them.

They arrived at my office early one morning, bringing hugs and tears somehow different from those we'd known just months before. In some ways, the three of us seemed transformed, but what exactly those changes were, it would be difficult to say; they were still the salt of the earth and I was still me. Yet there was something. . . .

"It's been difficult," Ruth said. "I can't believe I'm actually surviving this and yet life just goes on. One of our hopes, while we're in the area, is to find the right headstone for Amanda's grave. But this too has been difficult. We just haven't been able to find one that feels right and, believe me, we've searched. She was so young and the stones we looked at were all just too . . . hard."

John took Ruth's hand before he spoke. "We must have looked at every headstone in the state of Virginia and half of New York. We'd just like to find one that doesn't make us feel worse about what's happened."

I saw it instantly in my mind, clear as a bell, as if Amanda herself was standing in front of me: a little girl with her arms extended, a bird in her hands. I told Ruth and John that I was sure they'd find what they were searching for soon and not to settle. And one final time, I heard myself point out the obvious. "Your love for Amanda is eternal, and she is with you."

That afternoon they resumed their search and, at their first stop, found the perfect gravestone. It was a small bench, the size a child would use. Attached to it was a little girl holding a dove in her hands.

I don't know how many months passed, but it was a significant amount of time before I heard from Ruth again. She called to tell me how she and John, with a great deal of difficulty, had decided to donate all the gifts from Amanda's last Christmas to the children's ward where their daughter had once been a patient. Dropping the toys and stuffed animals off, she found herself surrounded by ailing children and their struggling families.

"It felt good to give those toys away," she said. "And while I was there, I had the opportunity to speak with parents of dying children, couples like John and me. It affected me to see them hurting so much, and it also seemed somehow redundant, as though they were re-crying our tears. So, I got this idea that maybe I could pass on some of what I learned."

"What a wonderful idea."

The months passed and Ruth seemed to gain strength each time I heard from her. She, indeed, started giving lectures and writing articles, offering help and guidance to the parents of dying children. As it turned out, she was exceptionally good at it. She recently said to me, "In the process of remembering Amanda, maybe that's what it does; it helps us understand not only our everyday muddied, patty-cake lives, but it helps us remember our own transcendence. I'm not sure how. I'm still puzzled about it. Of course, if I had my way, Amanda would still be here, but every now and then I lift up my eyes and say, 'Why me? How did I get this lucky?'"

31

Too much of a good thing is wonderful.

—Mae West

It is said that soon after his enlightenment the Buddha passed a man on the road who was struck by the Buddha's extraordinary radiance and peaceful presence. The man stopped and asked, "My friend, what are you? Are you a celestial being or a god?"

"No," said the Buddha.

"Well, then, are you some kind of magician or wizard?"

Again the Buddha answered, "No."

"Are you a man?"

"No."

"Well, my friend, then what are you?"

The Buddha replied, "I am awake."

–Kornfield

Carol and Kevin had lived next door for years. I passed them bleary-eyed in the driveway the day Ruth called to tell me Amanda had died. We had dinner together the week I first saw Margaret. Through all my encounters with the children and their parents, they were never far, a warm and welcome diversion, outside the sphere of my office, an island of normalcy. We were neighbors.

We had a dinner date one evening and another couple was to join us but, throughout the afternoon, I had the nagging sense it wasn't going to happen the way we'd planned. I told my boyfriend, "It's going to end up with just Carol and Kevin tonight. I don't know why, but I'm certain it's going to be just the four of us." Sure enough, at the last minute the other couple called to say they couldn't make it, and we changed the reservation from six to four.

The plan was to have dinner and catch a movie, but the

meal took longer than expected so we ended up skipping the movie and settling into a more leisurely pace. For as long as I'd known them, Carol and Kevin had been trying to have a baby. They tried in-vitro, the gift program, surgeries, fertility drugs, everything they could think of. None of it ever worked. In the end they decided on adoption, but even this avenue was blocked by a series of unreturned phone calls, missed opportunities, and unworkable matches. It was nearly Christmas, and they were both at the lowest point I'd ever seen them.

Carol and I spoke on a regular basis and I was aware of the pain and frustration she was feeling. I was certain she would get her baby, one way or another, but I was reluctant to tell her so directly—in case I was wrong. Kevin and I, on the other hand, hadn't spoken in several weeks and I was curious how this ongoing ordeal was affecting him. Toward the end of the meal, I asked him how he was doing and, to my surprise, he instantly opened up and began to recount emotionally the effect the last few years had had on him.

"I've always wanted to be a father," he confessed, "but lately I've been doubting myself. I'm not sure what I feel anymore. I think I'm just plain exhausted."

I reached over the table and touched his hand. "I think you may need some time for yourself."

"He has tons of time for himself," Carol jumped in.

"I mean time for himself where he's not trying to make everything work. Not trying to figure out how to get it right or perfect, or worrying about how to have a baby, or fix the car, or put food on the table."

Apparently this really hit home, because Kevin's eyes filled with tears and one even escaped down the side of his cheek. Carol had to turn away lest she break down herself.

"I can't remember ever having a moment when I felt everything was okay," Kevin said, "when there was nothing that needed doing."

I leaned across the table and placed my hand on Kevin's

heart. Right then, in that very moment, I knew that they were going to get their baby. I was absolutely certain of it. Later, when we were alone, I told my boyfriend, "It's going to happen soon. So soon, they won't have time to think about it."

The following morning, Carol called and excitedly asked if I wanted to go for a run. As we were jogging, she told me that the adoption agency called while we were out the night before. She could hardly get the words out. "Our profile has been picked. I can't believe it, Roseanne. We finally got our baby."

They named him Kevin Francis Joseph . . . after their dads.

And that was it; this simple, undramatic experience with Carol and Kevin somehow marked the end of one phase and the beginning of another. There would be no more Christmas babies. No more holiday angels. I didn't nearly understand the dynamics of it, but something had changed. Phones would still ring, car doors would slam shut, and little feet would crunch across gravel driveways. All that would be the same, but the calls weren't going to wait for Christmas or Thanksgiving or even Halloween anymore. They weren't going to wait for anything.

Several months later when the phone rang, I knew, before I answered it, that it was a mother. Her name was Linda and she said her six-year-old little girl, Jena, had an inoperable brain stem tumor. It felt like the last of autumn, but it was the third week of March.

And while the magic of the holiday phone calls ended with the arrival of Carol and Kevin's child, the year-round children are coming more frequently. Not only are there more of them, the original ones are still with me—even Matthew Henry, the baby I tried to hold through six inches of glass. His mother keeps me up to date on his life and I understand he's an active child, likes to play soccer and collect things. He's twelve years old now, blond and blue-eyed like his dad, with features like his mom. He worries a lot, and they say he's sensitive to everything. Apparently, since his recent entry into adolescence, he's been gripped by panic attacks. Years of playing hopscotch with the angel of death, only to live in constant uncertainty, has resulted for Matthew in paralyzing fear.

And why this family? Brian and Natalie had already paid; they went through three years of absolute hell after their son was born, with procedure after procedure, each trip to the neurosurgeon laced with the ever looming fear of a poor prognosis—a prognosis that, thankfully, never came. Matthew grew and the aneurysm steadily shrank, becoming less and less of a threat. It's still there but it hasn't changed in five years. Five years: a lifetime and a mere blink of an eye. Certainly not enough for the mother of any child.

Ten years ago, Natalie said to me, "I don't know what you did, but whatever it was, I believe it made a difference." Ten years ago, I reached for a deeply troubled child through a thick wall of glass, wondering why it had to be the way it was. The answer has not changed. It is simply because life matters; every tiny moment matters, the pulse of life and death continuing forever without willful control or imagined rules.

Yet until we are able to see the spirit in everything and grasp its essence, we can only work to understand the breath of it that is in each of us. And the more we understand and recognize the nature that is our own, the more we are filled with our selves, the more easily we can recognize another spirit without fearing it—even if it is a little girl who has decided to die.

1998

The runners looked shabby standing on the Verrazano Narrows Bridge. There were thousands upon thousands of them, all wearing outer clothing they would discard once the race began. The trick was not to shed too much too soon, or else risk being nipped by the cold morning air. Knowing the discarded clothing would be collected and distributed to the homeless, earlier in the week I had bought a heavy winter coat for ten dollars at the Goodwill store warm enough to withstand the sixty-minute wait for the start of the New York City Marathon.

Lynn was a marathon maniac; she had just completed two marathons on consecutive weekends and was in great shape. We'd been running together for years, usually five or six miles a day six or seven days a week, and she was rarely without a tale of her latest race, many of which took place in faraway, even exotic locales.

When the New York City Marathon was a couple of months away, Lynn was all excited about it; she'd run it for the last four years in a row and always had a great time. I said it sounded like fun.

"Run it with me this time."

"No way."

"Come on, it's not too late to get in race condition. You can train with me."

"I appreciate the offer, but no thanks."

Over the next several weeks, Lynn continued to tell me about her marathon experiences, recalling a different episode whenever we ran together. She routinely chanted, "You can do it, you can do it."

"No way," was my unwavering reply, "five miles a day is just fine for me. You marathoners are just plain crazy."

Day after day, run after run, she never let up. "Think about it, we'll have fun. It's the best, the most exciting. The New York crowds are fabulous. They'll carry you."

"No, thanks."

One morning, as I was returning from my daily five, Lynn appeared in her doorway in fresh running clothes, ready to start hers. "Come on, run with me. I'd love to have some company," she called to me.

"I just got back from a five-mile run. I don't know if I can do another five."

"Sure you can."

I ran another five miles with her, and it turned out she was right. It was not only easy, it was exhilarating, and the next time Lynn asked me to run the New York City Marathon with her, 26.2 miles seemed doable.

Scheduling the training runs was harder than the workouts, which went on for about eight weeks. We would run our normal five miles during the week and then increase the distance on Saturday or Sunday, taking the following day off. The first weekend we went ten miles, the next week fifteen, then eighteen. The weekend before the race, we dropped back down to fifteen miles after having peaked at twenty-four. Twenty-four miles, imagine that.

The New York City Marathon takes place the first Sunday

in November, so there was good reason to be concerned about the weather. I'd been experimenting with different outfits throughout training, trying to find one that didn't chafe or encumber yet could stand up to the cold. I kept an eye on the weather reports all week long and set aside different outfits for different conditions, praying it wouldn't rain.

It was six in the morning when Lynn and I boarded the specially chartered bus. There was a warming sense of camaraderie among the passengers, many of whom were marathon veterans. Someone asked if this was my first time and it ignited a storm of anecdotes and advice. In the midst of it, an enthusiastic racer asked if I was going to put my name on my shirt and I said I hadn't planned on it. Upon hearing this, she became insistent, saying I'd regret it if I didn't do it. Using a fabric marker, Lynn started writing out R-O-S-E-A-N-N-E in three-inch block letters on the front of my shirt.

It was barely 9 A.M. when we got off the bus and joined the massive crowd of people. Going with the flow, we registered, stashed our gear, and took one final pit stop. The event was amazingly well organized, although the lines at the five hundred portable toilets were long with anxious runners. An announcement was made that we should line up in our chosen category: the men's start, the women's start, or the coed start. Lynn and I were in the coed start on the bridge high above the harbor, the wind whipping around as we tried to loosen up. Several runners were dressed in Halloween costumes. It was an enormous party.

The race was about to begin, and runners started removing their outer clothing, shaking off the sting of the wind. Moments later, with New York City fireboats pumping out a towering display of red, white, and blue waters in the harbor below, Mayor Giuliani announced the start of the race. Although I didn't hear the gun go off, somebody yelled out that the race had begun, and there was a huge roar.

Then we stood still for the next ten minutes.

It took almost the entire length of the bridge before there

was enough distance between runners to break into a jog and not until the off-ramp came into sight were we in full stride. I asked Lynn if she thought we were going too fast too soon and she said it was just starting-gun adrenaline.

There was a distance marker and race clock at the end of the bridge and I was surprised to find we'd already run two miles. Moments later, we left the bridge and turned a corner where a wave of sound, the like of which I'd never heard before, met us as we came down the street: Brooklyn. Hundreds of voices melted together into a kind of roar, simultaneously encouraging and comforting. Two words rose above the din of the crowd: "Go, Roseanne!"

I stopped dead in my tracks and searched the faces that lined both sides of the street for the one that knew me. Lynn came up beside me, cracking up.

"What?"

She pointed to my shirt.

"Oh."

"You're going to hear your name shouted a lot over the next twenty-four miles. Is this wild or what?"

I had never heard anybody cheer for me before.

Go, Roseanne!

Go, Lynn!

Mile after mile, the race was everything Lynn had described: exhilarating, poignant, overwhelming. We stopped, took pictures, and danced to the music of every band we came upon, every imaginable type of music. Little children held out their hands for high fives as we passed, and I touched every one I could reach, my hand turning beet red.

"You'd better conserve your energy," the man running next to me cautioned.

I thanked him for the advice. "You're probably right, but I'm having the time of my life."

I ran close to the curb and outstretched hands for most of the race.

"Lookin' good, Roseanne," a thick New York accent encouraged.

"Thank you!" I shouted back into the crowd.

We were ten miles into the race before I knew it. My race set no world record, but I felt great. I'd been told that the typical goal of first-time marathoners is to finish in approximately five hours. My goal was to finish, to finish healthy, and to have a good time. When I pulled my hamstring muscle, my initial reaction was surprise, immediately followed by panic, followed by pain. At the next water station, I accepted the ibuprofen the volunteers were handing out.

The next seven miles flew by. The crowds, ten people deep, were loud with enthusiasm. In mile eighteen, we started up what looked like an endless incline, its crest nowhere in sight.

"How long is this hill?" I asked Lynn.

"About a mile."

Less than a minute later, I asked, "How much farther?"

"We're almost there," she replied.

"It feels like it will never end."

"We're through the worst of it."

Five minutes later, we reached the top of the hill and Lynn said, "It's downhill from here."

I hadn't mentioned the hamstring but it was starting to bother me. By the time we made it to the northern edge of Central Park and entered the final leg of the race, it was throbbing and my feet were burning. But there was no possibility I wasn't going to finish. Entering the park, the crowds were the biggest, loudest, and most enthusiastic yet and we began to pick up the pace. Go, Roseanne!

When we reached the last mile of the New York City Marathon, Lynn and I broke into a full sprint, running as fast as we could. She reminded me to look up at the finish-line clock where a camera recorded runner's final steps and official times. As I entered one of several cordoned-off lanes, Lynn entered another and we were separated by the huge bottleneck of racers. Volunteers instructed the finishers to keep their place in line and eventually the lane I was in narrowed to allow only one runner through at a time. A man came up from behind and tried to push ahead of me although the race was over. Maybe he was a little disoriented; I didn't know; our times had already been electronically recorded. I looked at him and said, "Stay in line."

"But my time," he pleaded.

"Everything's fine the way it is." I wasn't going to let him change anything.

When I reached the end of the line, a young woman draped a space blanket over my shoulders and placed a medal around my neck. She congratulated me several times and handed me a bottle of water and a small bag of goodies. Then, looking directly into my eyes, she hesitated ever-so-slightly before she placed a single long-stem red rose in my free hand. "It's all right," she said, "everybody cries at the end of the race."

The Monday after the marathon, every runner's name is printed in *The New York Times* and although you needed a microscope to find mine, there it was. Overall, I placed 19,122th out of 31,539. By gender I came in 3,780th out of 8,952. In my age group, I was 240th out of 760. My pace per mile was 10 minutes, 24 seconds. I finished the race in 4 hours and 33 minutes and 2 seconds. The number on my shirt was F3681, the name, Roseanne.

Afterword

The dove in downward flight is the symbol of the light and love of God, a love that never destroys and always connects. We do not have to be good or follow imaginary rules in order to qualify for that love; it's not a matter of us deserving it or having to earn it. The plan is firmly in place. We need only recognize that the dove is not on its way, it has already arrived. The flight is a bridge between the physical and the spiritual, between earth and heaven, bringing us deeper into our spirit, connecting us to every being in the universe, to the God that is the sum of all that is.

In this light, God is that which is present in the moment, where the lessons of yesterday no longer bind and the future has no existence, where the heart is open, and the soul spontaneously comes forth for the sake of its own fulfillment in the unpremeditated expression of life. This living pulse is an unstoppable force, natural and abundant, constant and forever flowing, enough for everyone, all the time, always available, always here. Here, where there are only miracles and nothing less, here where the Holy Mother comes to life every time our eyes meet, every time you take my hand, every time you understand my pain or I yours, every time we see each other as we are, free of judgment, criticism, and expectation to change.

There is grace in every moment that you care for me or I for you, in every cookie or flower or act of giving or receiving. The power of the word is in the physical manifestation of it. No matter what anybody says, no matter which books we read, no matter what suggestion or advice we receive, no matter how caring or well-intentioned the source, nothing compares to the touch of someone who cares, the look of acceptance in their eyes. That is God in our lives. The act of reaching for one another is the flight of the dove, the open heart of that yearning our sacred destination.

This is the song of children and it shall be sung forever. It is the song of Amanda, a little girl I met just once, and in whose clarity of life I found a new understanding of my own. I'm still in touch with Ruth, and once or twice a year I call her or she calls me, usually around Halloween or Thanksgiving. She recently sent me a copy of her latest published article. In it there's a picture of Amanda wearing little bib overalls atop a white puffy-sleeved shirt with a Peter Pan collar. She has one of the family's cats in a baby carriage and is petting him with both hands. She seems perfectly content. So does the cat. You can just make out the pattern on the wallpaper behind her. It has little hearts and tiny blue flowers on a white background.

Epilogue

The phone rang today. It was another mother, of course. She wasn't calling about a sick child, she was calling about herself. She wanted me to know she had just been diagnosed with a particularly devastating form of cancer. She didn't want me to save her. She just wanted my love. She had it. She was my mom.

The stories people tell have a way of
taking care of them. If stories come to
you, care for them. And learn to give
them away where they are needed.
Sometimes a person needs a story more
than food to stay alive.

—from *Crow and Weasel*
by Barry Lopez

References

Brennan, Barbara A. 1987. *Hands of Light: A Guide to Healing through the Human Energy Field*. New York: Bantam Books.

Bolen, Jean Shinoda, M.D. 1994. *Crossing to Avalon: A Woman's Midlife Pilgrimage*. San Francisco, Calif.: HarperSanFrancisco.

Bruyere, Rosalyn. 1987. *Wheels of Light: A Study of the Chakras*. Glendale, Calif.: Healing Light Center.

Klein, Josephine. 1987. *Our Need for Others and Its Roots in Infancy*. London and New York: Tavistock Publications.

Northrup, Christiane, M.D. 1998. *Women's Bodies, Women's Wisdom: Creating Physical and Emotional Health and Healing*. New York: Bantam Books.

Roth, Ron. 1997. *The Healing Power of Prayer: A Modern Mystic's Guide to Spiritual Power*. New York: Harmony Books.

Schwarz, Jack. 1978. *Voluntary Controls*. New York: Dutton.

Tansley, D. V. 1972. *Radionics and the Subtle Anatomy of Man*. Rustington, England: Health Science Press.

———. 1987. *The Raiment of Light: A Study of the Human Aura*. London, England: Arkana.

Whyte, David. 1992. *Fire in the Earth*. Langley, Washington: Many Rivers Press.

Endnotes

HOPE: Chapter 3

1. To "chelate" derived from the Greek word chele, or "claw," which means to claw out. Rev. Rosalyn Bruyere, who founded and developed this technique, adapted this word to mean simply to clear the field of the patient by removing auric debris. Chelation also fills up the aura with energy . . . and generally balances it. This is done by running energy into the body in steps starting at the feet (Brennan 1987, 205).

2. "The field of the child is entirely open and vulnerable to the atmosphere in which he lives . . . whether things are 'in the open' or not, the child senses what is going on. . . . The child's chakras are all open in the sense that there is no protective film over them which screens out the incoming psychic influences. This makes the child very vulnerable. . . . At around the age of seven, a protective screen is formed over the chakra openings that filter out a lot of the incoming influences. . . ." (Brennan 1987, 64).

HOPE: Chapter 8

1. Each of the seven chakras has a particular way of transforming energy the solar plexus chakra deals with emotional and physical energy, pain, and pleasure (Schwarz 1978, 87).

2. This technique is taught in the *Barbara Brennan School of Healing Sophomore Class Workbook*. Copyright © by Barbara Brennan, Inc.

CHARITY: Chapter 13

1. "Our body's energy system is always changing, and the potential for healing or disease is present at all times" (Northrup 1998).

Hampton Roads Publishing Company

. . . for the evolving human spirit

Hampton Roads Publishing Company
publishes books on a variety of subjects including
metaphysics, health, complementary medicine,
visionary fiction, and other related topics.

For a copy of our latest catalog,
call toll-free, 800-766-8009,
or send your name and address to:

Hampton Roads Publishing Company, Inc.
1125 Stoney Ridge Road
Charlottesville, VA 22902
e-mail: hrpc@hrpub.com
www.hrpub.com